Bobbin Lace Making

Opposite: 1. A Flemish Pillow

Bobbin Lace Making

DOREEN WRIGHT

BELL & HYMAN LONDON

Published by
BELL & HYMAN LIMITED
Denmark House
37–39 Queen Elizabeth Street
London SE1 2QB

First published in 1971 by
G. Bell & Sons Ltd
Reprinted 1972, 1976, 1979
Revised edition 1983

British Library Cataloguing in Publication Data
Wright, Doreen
Bobbin lace making. —2nd ed.
1. Bobbin lace
1. Title
746.2′22 TT805

ISBN 0 7135 1358 6

Diagrams by Hilary Evans

Printed in Great Britain by
Fletcher & Son Ltd, Norwich and bound by
Richard Clay (The Chaucer Press) Ltd,
Bungay, Suffolk

Contents

The Photographs

My thanks are due to Heather Wingrove for translating my handwriting into readable typescript.

D.W.

2. Venetian Gros Point needle made lace

O, fellow, come, the song we had last night.
Mark it, Cesario, it is old and plain;
The spinsters and the knitters in the sun
And the free maids that weave their thread with bones
Do use to chant it . . .

Twelfth Night, Act II, Scene 4

1. *The Story of Lace*

Before commencing a craft it is interesting and helpful to know at least a little of its history, from whence it came, how it has developed and how it has been affected by changes of custom, geography, history and climate. Earliest records of knotted fringe and pulled linen decoration are found in the wrappings of Egyptian mummies and on old Greek statues. The needle-point laces developed from these, becoming divorced from the linen material as the designs got more complicated until Venetian Gros Point reached its ultimate beauty about the time of the Renaissance.

As the demand changed from heavy ecclesiastical, processional uses to the lesser requirements of personal use on finer materials, so the character of the lace was adapted through 'Punto in Aria', Reticella, Rose point and Coraline point. As the habit of rich adornment of the person spread from Italy through France and to the Low Countries it became possible to spin very much finer threads in these damper climates and the techniques began to change. The brides – or bridges – made of button-holed bars between the major shapes of flowers and foliage, came to be replaced by net made by hooking on threads wound on bobbins, which were plaited into bars or twisted into a net. At first the needle-point patterns were used until it was found that even the flowers and leaves could be made with the bobbins and gradually the designs changed from heavy shapes assembled into a decorative whole to almost a fabric in which the net grounds with spots, sprigs and running trails came off the pillow as a complete entity all woven in together.

A study of paintings will show the uses to which the various forms were put and how the patterns have travelled from country to country.

The techniques came to be developed in different ways in various areas, and laces thus came to be affected by history and named after the place of manufacture. In

1569 the Duke of Alva's campaign in the Low Countries drove the independent burghers to board deep-bottomed boats in the deep rivers in which they were able to flee down Channel and land on the shores of Devon where the lace they brought, now known generally as Brussels, took root and is even to this day alike in pattern, technique, bobbins, pillows, decline and recovery. It came to be called 'Honiton' after the coach which brought it to London. The Massacre of St Bartholomew in 1572 brought the Huguenots to the shores of the Channel, where they boarded smaller boats on the shallow beaches and took the shortest route across to England. A coarse lace was being made here, but the French influence was felt through Sussex, Hampshire, Buckinghamshire, Bedfordshire and further north. In Bucks it really took root and 'Bucks Point Ground' laces in their heyday are as beautiful as Chantilly, Lille and Mechlin from which they are descended. A fresh infusion came as a result of the French Revolution.

In the latter part of the last century the fine old lace went into decline just about the time that a demand arose for a coarser lace for the calico petticoats of a growing lower middle class. This was met by a quicker-moving lace using cheaper, coarser cottons based on Maltese, Torchon and Cluny patterns, often all mixed together, in a way my old teacher used to call 'Bastard Maltese'. Some of this lace is often called 'Bucks' but is more truly 'Beds', where a great deal was made.

Thus the main bobbin laces fall into three groups, each with a geographical title of origin.

A.	Brussels and Honiton	Pillow-made sprigs, leaves, etc., joined with bobbin net or needle point, or appliquéd on to machine-made net.
B.	French, Bucks	Lille, Chantilly, Mechlin. Fine net with sprigs, etc., in cloth work surrounded by a thicker thread called a gimp or trolly woven into the piece, coming off the pillow complete.
C.	Torchon, Cluny, Maltese, Bedfordshire	A coarser lace with 'Tallies', leaves, plaited bars, various whole stitch and $\frac{1}{2}$ stitch nets.

All the above laces are made on a *pillow* of some sort. The *pattern* is pricked out on parchment or card which is firmly pinned to the pillow. The *thread* is wound on bobbins which are hung in pairs on *pins* stuck in the pricking. The bobbins are then crossed and twisted according to the pattern below them, the pins being stuck as required between the bobbins to keep the threads in their place. About 2″ or more of new pinning up are done before taking any pins from the back and using on the new work. The speed of work, of course, varies with the width and complication of the pattern and the skill of the worker. A simple first or second

Diagram 1. Uses of lace illustrated in paintings

3. Honiton. Photograph shows wrong side as worked on pillow. Whole and $\frac{1}{2}$ st rose petals. Tallies or 'leadworks' in flower centre. Picot bars and raised work on leaves.

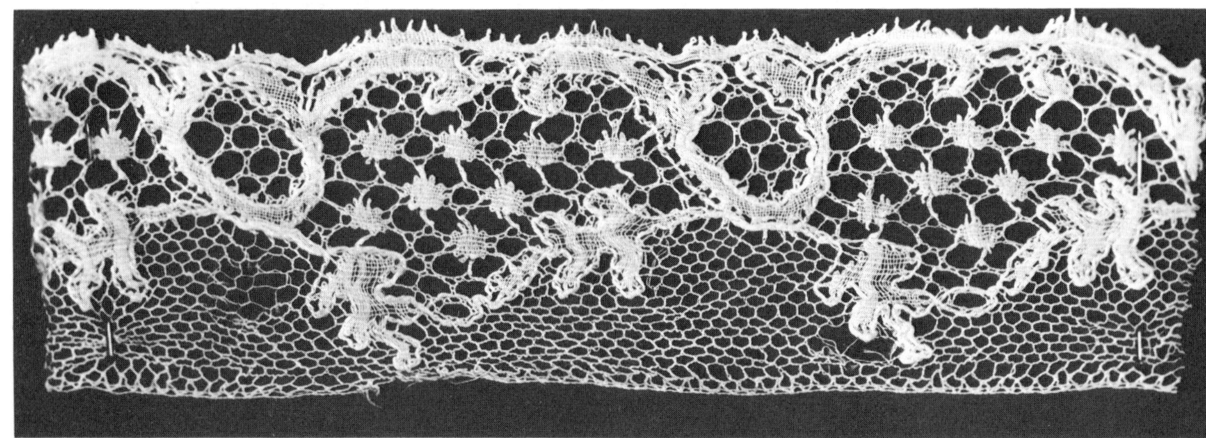

4. Old Bucks Point or Lille, showing Mayflower in Hc at Head

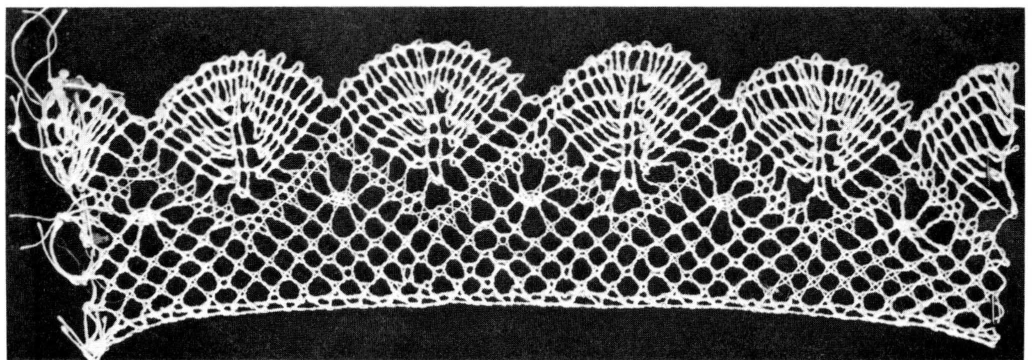

5. Torchon

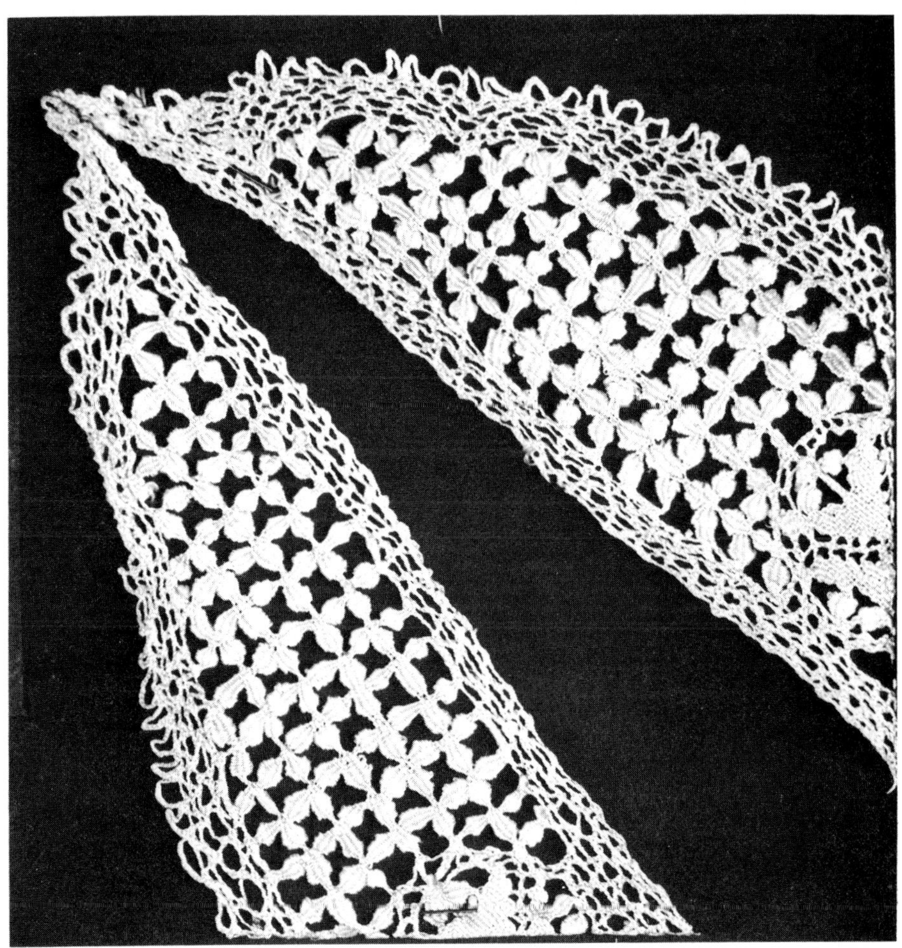

6. Maltese

7. Cluny. N.B. Single thread purls which do not hold their shape in wear and washing.

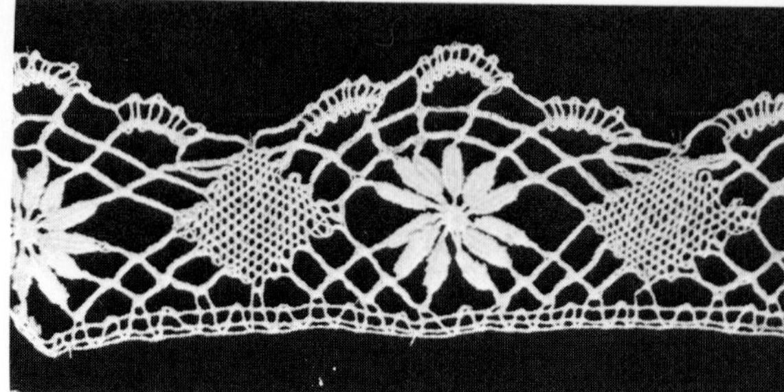

8. Beds

pattern should move at the rate of 3 or 4 'heads' an hour before a more complicated one is tried.

The craft could be used more often for remedial therapy as, apart from the good exercise of the fingers, it is an extremely refreshing occupation requiring more concentration than knitting or similar pastimes and therefore taking the mind off the worries of a household, business or family. I always get up from half an hour's lace making refreshed and ready for the next dull chore. It is not nearly as difficult as it looks with its cluster of tightly ranked pins. The pattern is there beneath the threads and the scale of working is the full spread of the bobbins on the pillow. The required pin hole can almost be felt if it cannot be seen. The author has known many old people aged eighty to ninety who were still happily lace making and has personally found the craft much less of an eyestrain than pulled linen or counted thread. In the lace schools of the last century children used to attend from the age of four to learn the craft with their numbers and letters. If they could not produce a saleable edging by the age of seven they were apprenticed to another trade. So it is learnable by even the youngest, is enjoyable for all ages, and the product can become an heirloom of lasting joy and beauty.

Twenty pins have I to go
Let ways be ever so dirty
Never a penny in my purse
But farthings five and thirty.
Old Lace Tell

2. *Requirements of the Craft*

PILLOWS

Lace is made on a *pillow* which can be of almost any shape provided it is stuffed very hard and covered with a firm material so that a pin stuck upright can have a pair of bobbins hung round it without displacement on pulling. Instructions for making pillows with illustrations are given in Appendix A but listed here are some of the traditional ones which can often be bought or borrowed by beginners.

a. *Flat* or board based. Simple to make but of limited use after the beginning. The Devon pillow is like this but round and higher.
b. *Bolster*. Easily made and usually used for narrow edgings and Torchon laces. Requires a long pricking or two lengths to leapfrog. Rather bulky in use and must have some sort of stand or box to prevent it rolling over.
c. *French*. A mini bolster inserted into a cushion on which the bobbins are spread. It is practical and easily stored.
d. *Swiss or Dutch*. As above, built on a frame but instead of a bolster has a channel down the middle with 3 flat square cushions which can be moved up as the lace progresses and turned round to facilitate corner turning. See title page.

CLOTHS

The pillow should have a washable cover well secured on the pillow or even completely enclosing the whole. The pricking should be backed with a band of dark material at least 1″ wider each side. The 'working cloth' is then pinned on over the part of the pricking not being used, large enough to reach from side to side of the pillow, on which the bobbins will be spread, and long enough to reach to the bottom of the pillow and double back over the bobbins and work. A final

9. A collection of bobbins

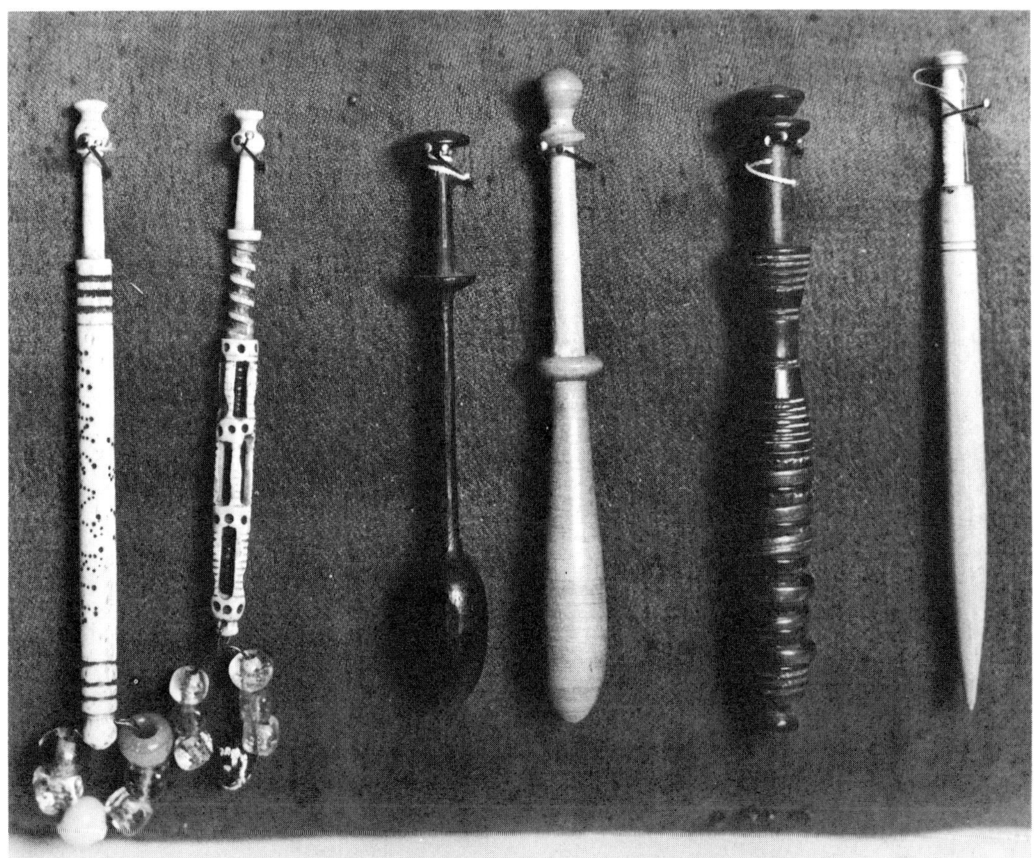

10. *Left to right:* two Jingles, two French, 'Thumper', Honiton

dust cover is required to keep the whole clean at all times and should be replaced even during temporary short absences, such as when answering the telephone. It is quite extraordinary how soon lace, left open to the air, gets that 'antique' shade that really indicates dirt.

BOBBINS

Workers usually pride themselves on the collection of antique bobbins on their pillows. As collectors move in on these items many will have to 'make do' with modern equivalents. The three basic varieties are known as 'Jingles', 'Thumpers' and 'Frenchies'. Basically, if fine lace is being made, a bobbin is required having a weighted end which, in being moved over the pillow, helps to keep a good tension without having to be picked up and pulled tight, which would tend to break the thread. Therefore I advise 'Jingles', wooden or bone. The rings of beads, besides giving the weighting required, do not get so muddled on being pushed over to the side and do incidentally look lovely on the pillow. The next best are the 'Thumpers' which are wooden with rings of pewter or brass round the handle. The 'Frenchies' are adequate and quite good tools but best suited to Torchon and Cluny only. Modern turned wood and plastic bobbins can now be bought. They can also be fairly easily made with a penknife out of thin soft wood dowelling rod. The hole for the bead ring can be drilled or burnt out. Honiton bobbins have no bob or spangled end but a point to enable the bobbin to be passed through a loop during 'sewings'. A few larger bobbins are needed on which are wound thicker gimp threads.

The PRICKING or PATTERN

This must be on firm card of a tight texture or on parchment. The Pricker can be made from dowelling with a No. 9 needle for pricking off from old parchments, but a No. 8 fits modern pins better. It must always be used vertically.

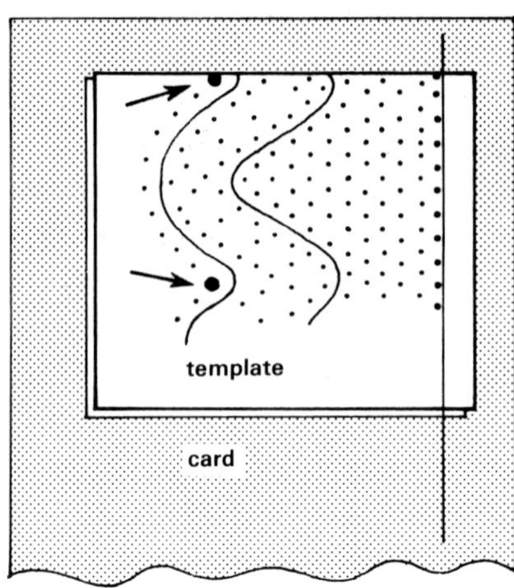

Diagram 2. The pricking or pattern. Pricking *must* be done on a flat surface. A cork mat or 1-inch close-grained polystyrene, which gives a more accurate deep hole, are ideal.

Collect patterns by borrowing and pricking off at least two repeats. When pricking a length of pattern score with your pricker a ruled straight line on your pricking card, on which the outside foot pin holes will be pricked, and a similar straight line through the foot pin holes of the template or sample piece. Choose also one prominent pin hole on the head side at junction of heads. Be sure that these coincide or the resulting lace made on your pricking will not be straight. Teachers usually supply photostat copies for their pupils. One must use these for quite a while and learn to understand them before attempting to prick off from a treasured pricking and, maybe, ruin it. See Appendix B for designing your own patterns, enlarging from old or too small patterns.

PINS

Pins must always be of brass or white metal and *never* of steel. I have seen so much new and antique lace ruined by iron mould from steel pins. They should be fine and as long as possible. If coarse, they not only wear out the pricking but tend to cause difficulties and sore fingers from fitting too tightly in the holes.

THREAD

Thread must be of a thickness to suit the pricking on which it is to be used. Since the formation of the Lace Guild in 1976 many more people stock the required thread supplied by manufacturers who have been persuaded to make it, even going as far, in one instance in Belgium, as to re-open a closed wing.

The only way to test the thread is on a length of foot braid, where it must lie flat and fill the space, allowing for the twists each side at the pin holes. It must not crinkle or have to be pulled straight as this would give a 'crèpy' look to the lace. If in doubt, use the finer of the threads between which you are choosing.

Numbers given to threads are very confusing as they tend to vary not only from one manufacturer to another but even amongst threads from a single manufacturer's list. This makes it essential that you try out a new thread before using it.

Honiton needs a very fine thread usually described as 'Egyptian Gassed Cotton'. It has been flamed to get rid of whiskers. It comes in 120/2, 140/2 and 160/2.

For making other types of lace you have a wide choice of thread. DMC No. 30 Retors D'Alsace works well for most Torchon and Bedfordshire laces but the finer ones require No. 40 or No. 50. But DMC Cordonnet Special No. 150 is a fine crochet or tatting thread and is too round and hard for bobbin lace. Copley Marshall No. 120, a mercerised cotton, can be used for coarser Honiton, fine Bucks and Tönder.

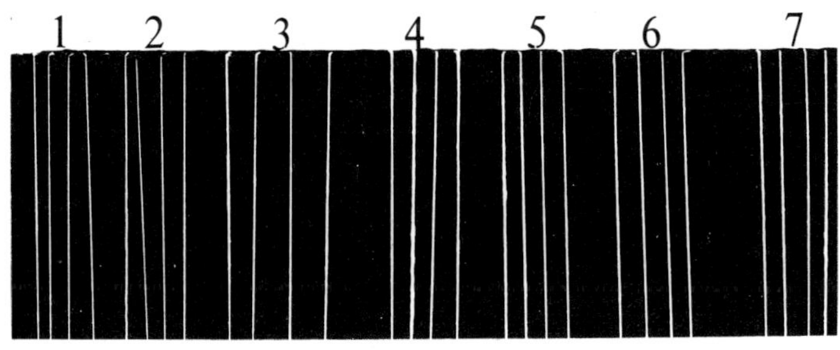

1. Cotton, gassed, 180
2. Cotton, gassed, 140
3. Irish flax 200
4. Bouk Belgian thread 150
5. Bouk Belgian thread 120
6. Belgium cotton 120
7. Swedish flax 100

11. Thread gauge (actual thicknesses)

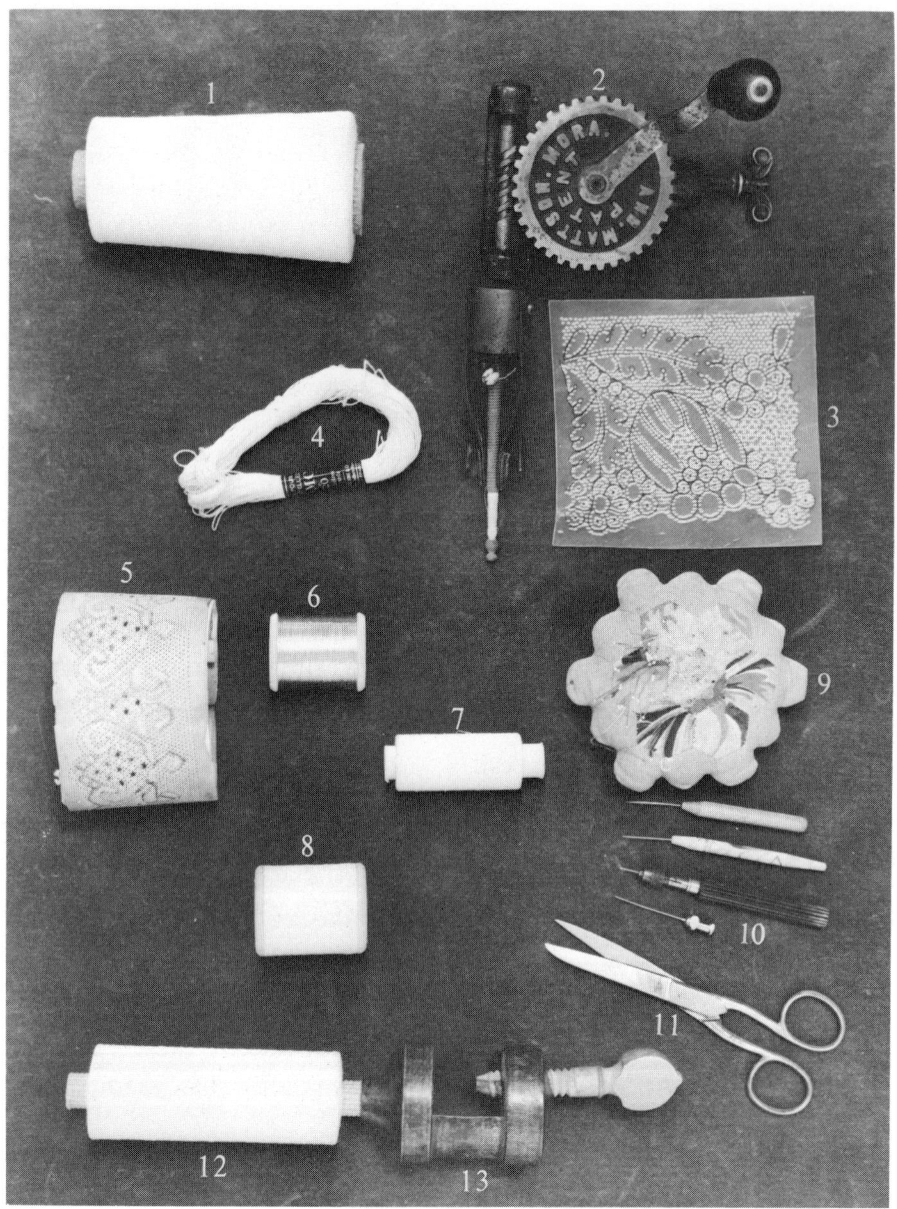

12. Various needs for lace making including spools of threads from various sources

1. Belgium. 2. Winder (clamps on to table edge). 3. Pricking 'template', i.e. complete repeat. 4. Gimp thread D.M.C. No. 5. Old parchment pricking. 6. Gold thread. D.M.C. OR MI-FIN No. 10. 7. Devon thread 140. 8. Knox 'Falcon' 150. 9. Pincushion. 10. Various prickers. 11. Scissors – sharp but with handle bent for tying off. 12. Devon thread 180. 13 Reel holder. (Nos. 4 and 8 are not currently available, but similar threads are.)

For a pricing on $\frac{1}{10}$-inch or 2-mm graph paper, you need a DMC No. 60 thread or finer. An alternative to DMC No. 60 is English Sewing Thread 'Unity' Nos. 80 and 150.

In fact the choice is now very wide in white, ecrue, half-bleached, linen and cotton threads. The latter is smoother as modern methods of manufacture and the type of flax available make it difficult to get a very fine unslubbed linen thread. Experiments are being done with man-made fibres in the more modern laces but they do not hold a picot well or work flat in traditional laces because they tend to stretch.

Parts of the pattern in the French, Buckinghamshire and Danish laces are outlined with a 'Gimp' or 'Trolley' (Danish Trolle). This should be a round *shiny* thread of sufficient thickness to form a definite *contrast* with that of the rest of the lace. If it is too close in thickness it tends to give the lace a muddled look instead of emphasizing the outlined shape. DMC Coton Perle and similar threads are now used and must be three or four times thicker than the lace threads. I use as a Gimp No. 8 with No. 50, 60 or 100 thread, No. 12 with No. 120 and beyond. The 'coarse cotton' in Honiton is usually No. 50 Coats machine thread.

One also needs a variety of boxes for keeping bobbins in, separating the bobbins with different thread thicknesses wound on and some sort of case for your prickings. A *winder* is useful but not necessary until large numbers of bobbins are required for major works.

The last requirement but by no means the least important is a comfortable seat with the pillow in such a position that the work may be seen without the necessity of stooping over it and thus causing neck and shoulder aches. A flat type of pillow could be on a table like a typewriter. A high bolster type may be held on the lap, leaning against the table edge or against the back of a chair, the lower rung of which forms a convenient foot-rest. The writer uses a low armless fireside chair with her French pillow on a cushion on her lap. If any strain is felt across the back, neck or shoulders try raising the height of the pillow in relation to the eyes. Slightly raising the back often is all that is necessary but do not make the pillow so steep that the bobbins tend to roll in a heap to the front. They *must* be able to hold their positions spread out.

Nineteen miles to the Isle of Wight
Shall I go there by candle light?
Yes, if your fingers go lissom and light
You will go there by candle light.
Old Lace Tell

3. *First steps*

Winding the Bobbins and Making a Braid

Select pairs of bobbins to wind for a braid, using your bigger bobbins in order to take thick, coloured threads as it will be found helpful for a beginner to have these colours to guide her place-wise. Have 2 pairs in one colour for weaving, the workers, and lettered (*a*) (see Diagram 5), then have two more pairs each in two pleasantly contrasting colours, (*b*) and (*c*). The thread is wound firmly and flatly clockwise round the bobbin when the *head* is facing directly towards you. The correct way to have a pair wound is to wind enough for two on to one bobbin and then wind off on to the second. This avoids a knot but is tedious so most lacemakers fill two bobbins and join them with a closely trimmed *reef knot*. There

Diagram 3. Winding a bobbin. The reef knot

is a 'weavers knot' that is good and flat but it can go wrong, is difficult to describe and teach, whereas a reef is easy to teach, easy to do and can be seen to be wrong if it is so when the little ends lie across the threads instead of along them. The knot is then wound a foot or two on to one of the bobbins. During the work this knot can often be buried in some weaving or 'taken out' by lifting the bobbin, taking it round a pin at the back and bringing it back into operation. Avoid, if you can, doing this anywhere in net areas, i.e. do it in plenty of time before that bobbin works in the net. Each thread is then held on the bobbin with a hitch which must be made so that the bobbin hangs firmly but more thread can be released with a slight turn of the bobbin to the left. To make this hitch, hold the bobbin in the right hand, grasp the thread end between the left little finger and its neighbour,

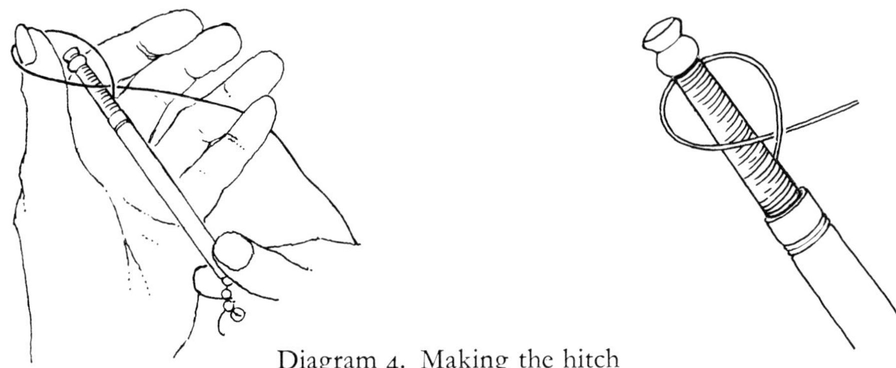

Diagram 4. Making the hitch

lift the thread by placing the left thumb on the thread, coming from the back, going under the thread, forward and up. Bring the head of the bobbin in front of the taut thread, round in towards the palm and up through the thumb loop. Pull firm.

Honiton workers wind the thread two or three times round the head knob before doing the hitch but I find it better to do the hitch round the wound thread as this holds firmer. If the thread has been wound firmly and regularly it should not bury itself. It is quite essential that the thread be wound on the right way and the hitch be made right. It then becomes quite automatic when requiring more length to dip the thumb to release more thread. If the head of the bobbin is raised slightly during this movement it makes it easier. Each pair is now hung on a pin on the back of the pillow ready for setting up the pattern. **During the winding and all through lace making it is essential to avoid touching the thread with the fingers.**

THE PRICKING FOR THE BRAID

With a length of 10 graph paper about 1″ wide and 10″ long pinned on to a similar size of pricking card, prick holes as shown, keeping the pricker absolutely perpendicular. The width apart of the holes can be varied according to the number and thickness of threads required as passives, i.e. those threads lying straight down.

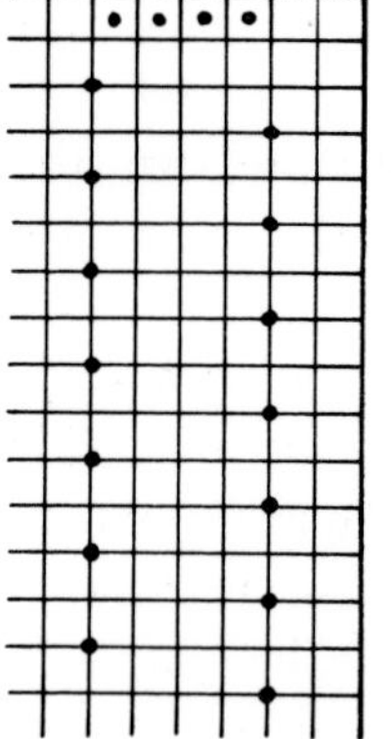

5*a*. Four pin holes for hanging on only N.B. Right side drops down one line

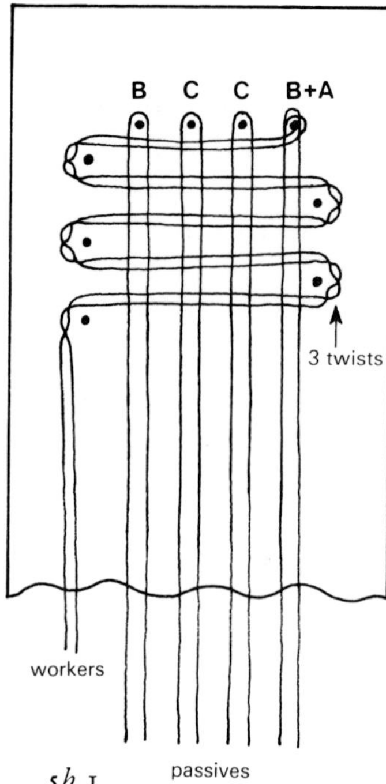

5*b* 1

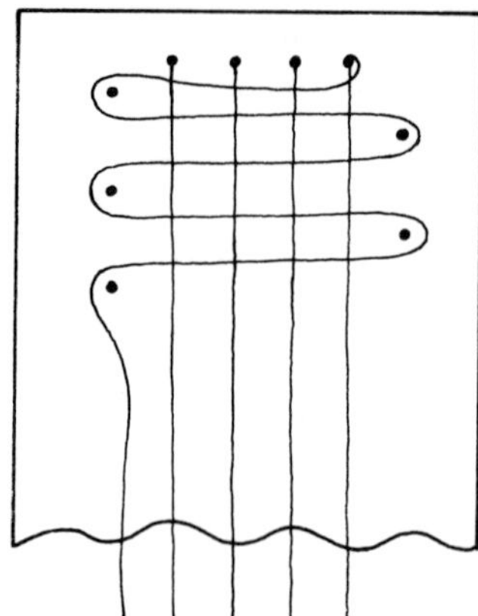

5*b* 2. For greater clarity in diagrams it is usual to show each pair as one line

Diagram 5. Pricking and weaving the braid

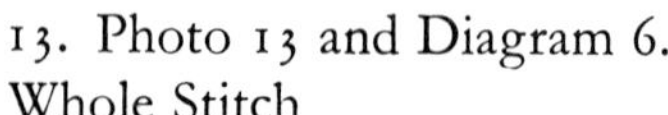

13. Photo 13 and Diagram 6. Whole Stitch

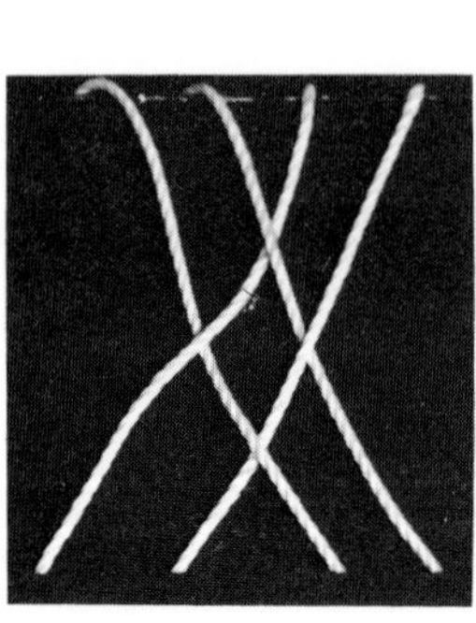

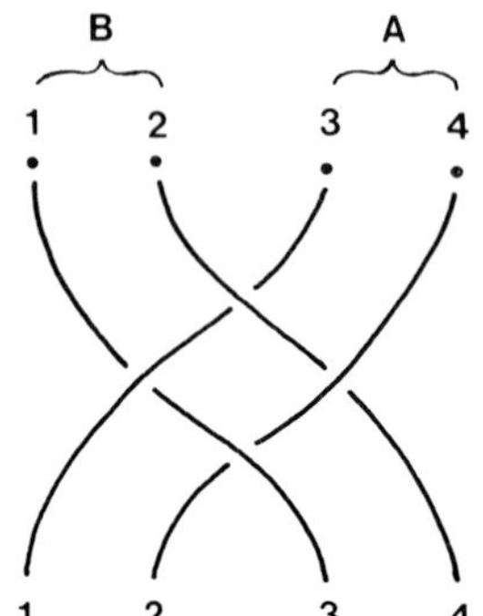

WHOLE STITCH

Using the pricked card, which must be firmly pinned on the pillow, hang the coloured pairs (*b*) and (*c*) over pins in the top row of holes and one of the (*a*) pairs over the right hand (*b*) pin. We now weave the (*a*) pair through the other pairs using *whole stitch* which is done as follows, remembering that *crossing* is left over right and *twisting* is right over left:

Taking pair (*a*) and pair (*b*) to the middle of the pillow imagine the *positions* are numbered as shown. Pick up 2 and *cross* over 3. Using both hands pick up 2 (previously 3) and 4 and *twist* over 1 and 3 (previously 2). Cross 2 over 3.

Note: Throughout this book 'Cross' means left over right and 'Twist' right over left.

The first pair (*a*) has thus been woven through the (*b*) pair and has thus changed positions. Throughout lace it is the *position* of *pairs* on the pillow that matters and not the whereabouts of individual bobbins. Having made this stitch the right-hand pair is pushed to one side and the next pair on the left (*c*) brought in to make the next whole stitch and so on through the other available pairs. The 'workers', which is the pair (*a*) that has come through, is then twisted three times and a pin put in the hole under it. This is called 'putting up a pin'. The workers are then taken back through the passives leaving the left-hand pair of each stitch as completed and bringing in the next on the right until all are done. Twist 3 times and pin up as before. These edge pins must be very slightly leaning outwards to keep the tension firm and all must lean at exactly the same angle as the pins above them.

This simple weaving stitch is the basis of all lace. Divide, halve it, add twists and all the beauty of lace grows from this seed.

Continue for a length until you can make the braid firm and even and the little loops each side are tidily straight.

We now learn to do a foot by adding in another (*a*) pair. The foot of lace consists of two passives, a worker and a twisted pair which joins the side loops on the right-hand side of lace, i.e. the *foot*. Weave through to the right, twist the workers 3 times, hang the new (*a*) pair on the workers, put the pin up and close round the pin. Using the left worker weave across to the left pin and back through

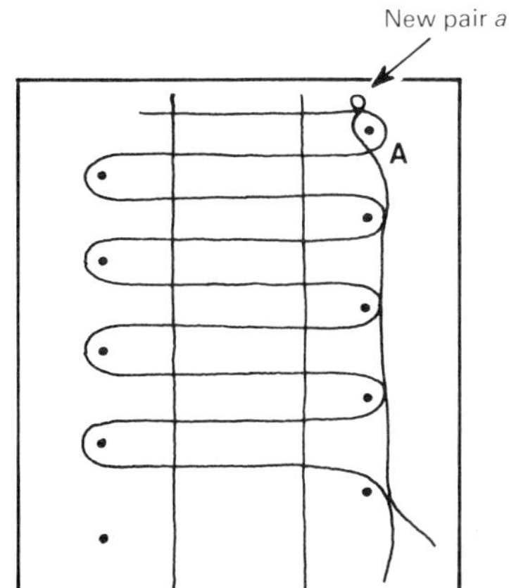

Diagram 7. Adding a foot pair

the last passive, twist three times, make a whole stitch with the other worker, twist both 3 times and *pin up under both* and repeat. It will be noticed that the working pairs change places after this operation. When making insertions this foot stitch is done on both sides of the lace.

Before discarding your braid pricking we learn *half stitch* by which an attractive little edging can be made. Half stitch is a more open kind of weaving that gives a lighter effect. It consists of:

HALF STITCH

Cross the middle bobbins, twist the side pairs, move out right pair, move pair in from left. Cross middle, twist sides, move out right pair and so on across to the pin hole, twist last left-hand pair, pin up and work back. This is often used instead of cloth work to give a lighter effect when required or as a contrast to whole stitch. It has a diagonal effect. To make the edging: work four pins down in whole stitch each side, then do four pins in half stitch and repeat.

NET GROUND

As in Bucks Point Ground, Paris point, Vrai reseau, Honiton net, Lille net.

The net or 'ground' is made by using a $\frac{1}{2}$ stitch with the side pairs twisted *three* times and putting up a pin between them. It is always worked on the diagonal with pairs coming out from the head and attached at the foot side at the 'catch' pin. The method will be described in the next chapter when we do 'Little Fan'.

Honeycomb will be dealt with before doing Pattern 2 – the 'Sheep's Head'.

This book has been designed as a progressive course, one pattern leading to the next and therefore avoiding too much repetition unless something is so important that it needs emphasis. Some of these are simple things, such as '*Cross* the gimps', that are easily forgotten. Some are things that are not easy to remember.

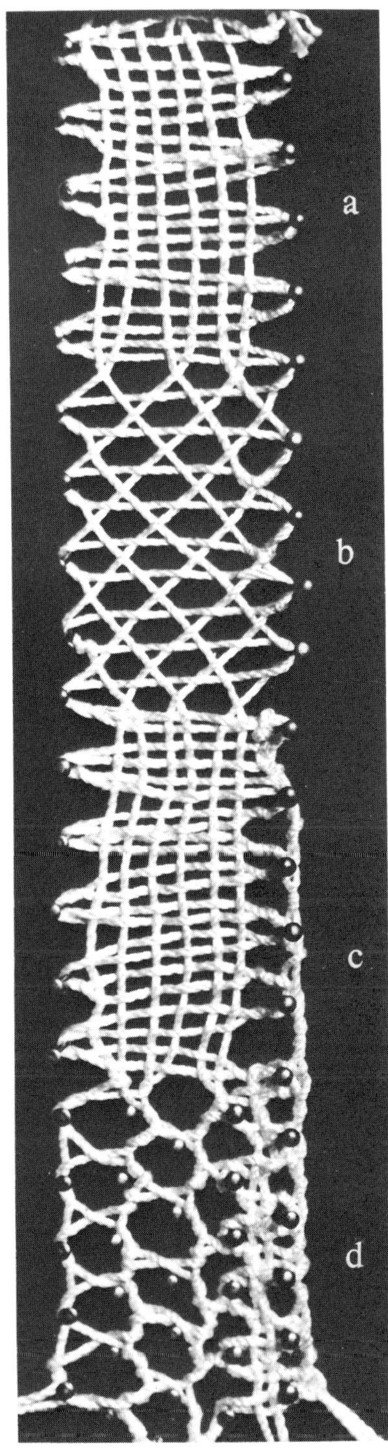

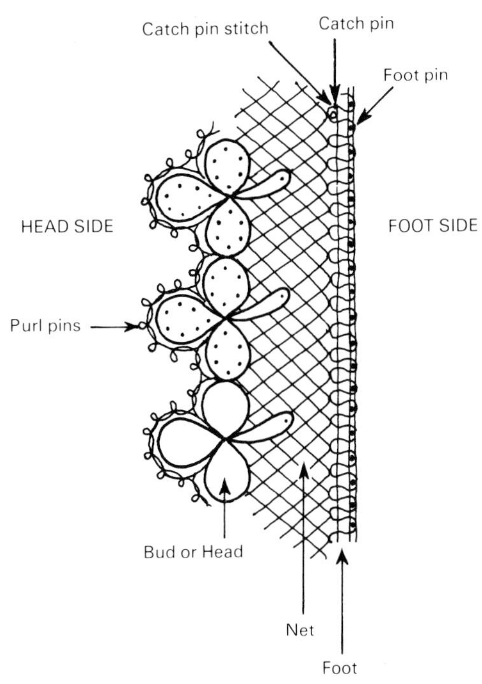

Diagram 8. The Geography of Lace

14

a Whole stitch braid

b Half stitch braid

c Foot

d Net

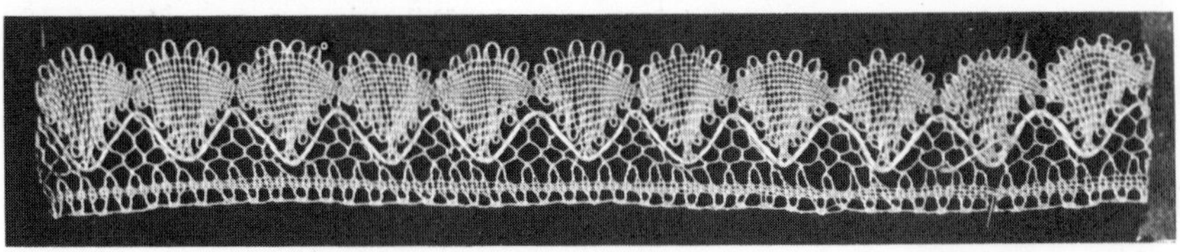

15. Little Fan

4. *Little Fan*

Abbreviations in this chapter:

wh st	whole stitch
prs	pairs
Tw3	twist three times
rt pr	right pair
lt pr	left pair

You need 12 prs of bobbins with 100 thread and one larger bobbin wound with a gimp thread.

Make your pricking following the chart. If you are using an old or borrowed one, check that it is for 'Lille' or 'Point' ground by looking at the pin holes on the net. They should be in a pattern of a diamond shape · ⁚ ·. If they are right-angled they will be for a Torchon fan ·⁚·. Draw in the gimp line on the pricking in indian or some other non-smudging ink. Even if you do not use a gimp at first it is helpful for defining the head and net areas. Pin the pricking firmly on the pillow with pins in the top corners and every three inches or so near the edges, driving them well home so as not to catch the threads moving over them.

SETTING UP

At A hang 4 prs on a pin. Taking the pr on the head side, twist 3 times (Tw3), then weave in whole stitch (wh st) through the other 3 prs, Tw3, hang a new pr on the twists, put pin in B, close round the pin with the new pr and the workers and work left to C, Tw3, pin up and work wh st back to D, Tw3, hang new pr on workers, pin up in D and continue through E, F, G and H which is the point of the fan. While doing this weaving, spread the bobbins widely on the pillow, making the

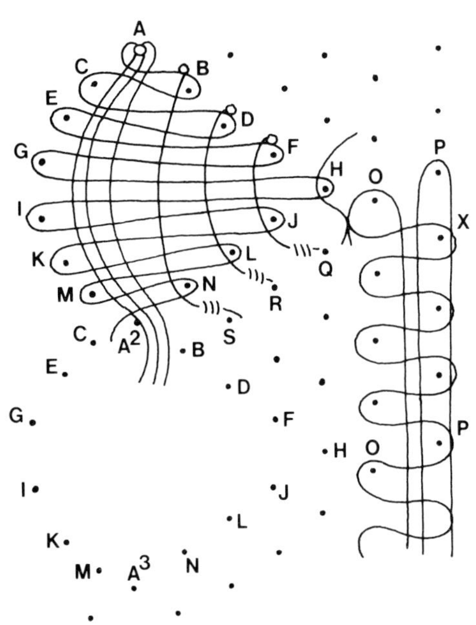

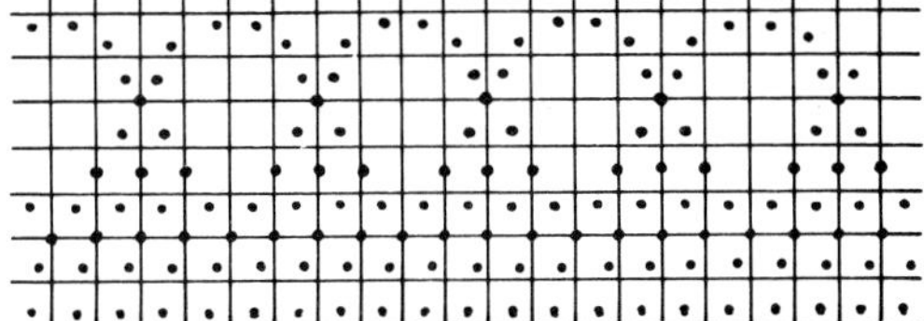

Diagram 9.
Chart and diagram for Little Fan

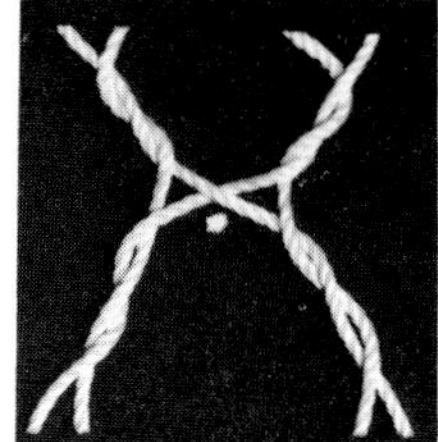

16. Net Stitch

stitch in a very open space in the middle. It is this movement of the bobbins to and fro which settles in the threads to an even weave and helps to fill the curve of the head, avoiding leaving long empty loops at the head pins. This head pin is usually referred to as a 'snatch' pin. From H the fan is decreasing so at H, J, L and N the rt pr, after closing round the pin, is twisted twice (Tw2) and left out ready for the net block. After closing round pin at N, weave through to A, Tw3, pin up under worker and leave until the net is done. Hang 2 prs on pins in O and P. It will be found helpful if the 2 inner prs hanging between O and P are the same sort of bobbin and rather distinctive from the rest of those on the pillow. They will be the passives in the foot braid. O is the catch pin and P the foot pin. With the lt pr on O, Tw3, and make a *net stitch* with the pr from H, i.e. *cross the middle two bobbins, twist the side prs 3 times*. This is the *catch-pin stitch* and does not have a pin put up between the prs. Take the left hand of these 2 prs and work a *net* stitch, with the pr from J, and pin up between them at Q. With lt pr from Q and pr from L make a net stitch and pin up at R and the same at S. It will be noted that when looking for the bobbins to work these net stitches they should be lying already twisted over the pin at the angle of the diamond already mentioned to the right and left of the pin hole to be worked. The movement of work must be on the diagonal descending from the foot to the next head. Now pass the worked net prs over to the left of the pillow with a mildly combing motion of the fingers which helps to keep them in order in prs and firms the tension without a pull. When you come to the catch-pin prs, i.e. where there are 2 prs hanging between the pins instead of 1 as in the net proper, take the right hand of these 2 prs, work to the right, wh st twice through the 2 passives, Tw3, wh st with the foot pr, Tw both 3 times and put up pin under both prs on the foot edge at X. Leave rt pr out, weave back through the 2 passive pairs, Tw3 and pin up at catch pin and then (not before) make the catch-pin stitch, work two net stitches with pins between, comb back as before, work foot, catch-pin stitch, and one net stitch. Work another foot and catch-pin stitch. Now comb the foot prs over to the right of the pillow, the catch-pin prs and those twisted prs from Z, Y and S. With the left hand of the catch-pin prs and these 3 from the net, you have 4 prs, all twisted, ready to go into the next head. The hanging on of 12 prs, and all stitches, are now complete.

At A2 weave to the rt through 3 passives, bring in the net pr from S, make wh st, twist rt pr 3, pin up, close round pin, weave to head, Tw worker 3, pin up and return and take in the pr from Y. Similarly down to the point (H) where the left-hand catch-pin pr comes in and immediately after closing round the pin goes out. When the head is completed the 4th pr from the foot above this hole H completes the foot by going right to the foot pin and working back to the next catch pin where it picks up this last head pr to make the catch-pin stitch before continuing with the top net line. This operation is an important one and must be firmly handled as a hole can come here, which spoils the appearance of the whole assemblage of head, net and foot.

THE GIMP

Work a length of the pattern and, when familiar with it, put in a gimp thread by attaching it to the pin at A, having completed a net block. Before beginning the head pass the gimp through the twisted prs to the *right* by placing it between the bobbins of each pr and bringing the *right-hand* bobbin *right* over the gimp and the left-hand one and twisting twice. At H, after completing the head, move the gimp to the *left*, place it between the bobbins of a pr, lift *left-hand* bobbin over gimp, dropping it to the *left* of its pr and twisting twice. Always have these twists each side of the gimp to secure it in the place you want it and check it is gently pulled into place on the corners before you turn the next. This single gimp does improve the edging by defining the head and net areas.

N.B.

1: Make sure your prs coming from the net ground are always twisted before making the next stitch.

2: The passives at the foot and the through threads of the head must always hang straight down without any twists.

3: The worker in the weaving should be kept as horizontal as possible in any pattern containing weaving.

4: Be very careful not to pull the foot passives or the foot pr tight as this would gather the lace or make it slightly curved when off the pillow. If you find you are pulling it too tight try making the last foot stitch a ½ stitch. But that method is not so strong and does not look as regular as a wh st.

5: Always twist the worker before putting up a pin round which it is going. Do not twist after pinning up.

6: Always spread your bobbins widely while working.

VARIATIONS

This edging may be varied by the head being worked in ½ stitch instead of wh st. Or by giving the workers one or two twists on each crossing between the 2nd and 3rd prs from the head a dainty little vein is made.

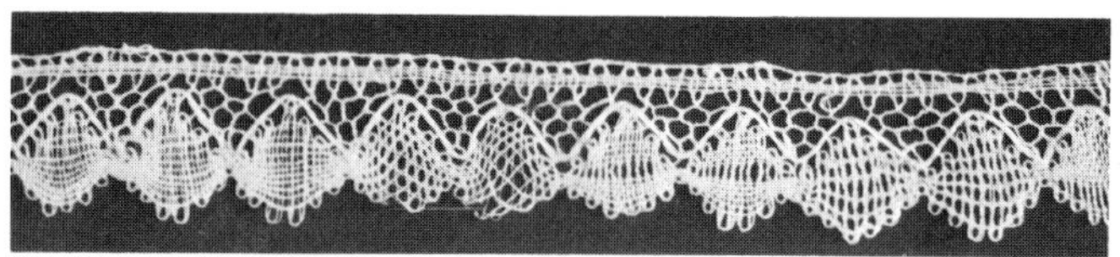

17. Little Fan Variations.
Left to right: 1–3 wh st, 4–5 ½ st, 6–7 vein, 8–9 1 Tw after each wh st of passives and workers

CUTTING OFF

What is done at the end of a piece of lace depends upon whether it is going to be joined on to the beginning of itself, as in a doyly or handkerchief (*a*), or (*b*) just finished off firmly for sewing on or into cloth or just to make an end.

(*a*) It is very important to begin lace correctly if the end is going to be joined to it, i.e. a neat row of loops over pins and a firm gimp. When the end has been reached and pattern matching well planned cut the bobbins off leaving 4″–5″ of thread. Cut them off in prs by means of a blunt or loosened pr of scissors.

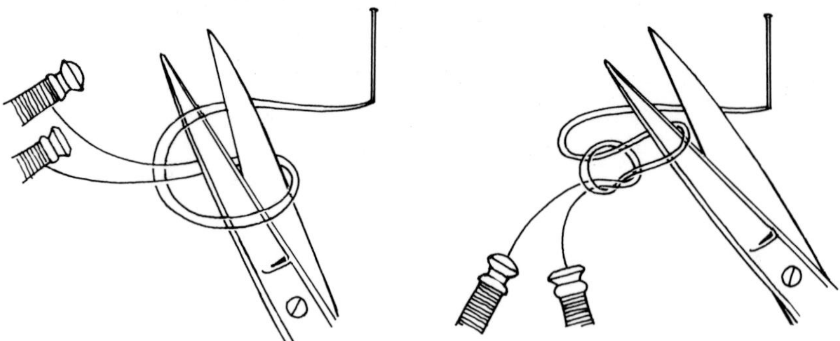

Diagram 10. Cutting off, or 'bowing out' the bobbins.

Holding the bobbins in your left hand place the scissors slightly opened on the 2 threads, twist down, back to you and up, catch the 2 threads on the lace side of the loop between the open jaws, pull through the loop, tighten and cut at the top of the loop. The 2 bobbins should then come out of the knot tied together ready for the next job.

When the bobbins are cut off and *not before* unpin the lace. On an empty pillow pin the beginning of the lace down by the head and foot, lay the end exactly over it, matching the pattern and put in 2 or 3 pins to hold in place. With the pricker pull one thread of each pr through its opposite equivalent loop and tie a reef knot with its partner. Cut off one thread and whip the other over three or four bars of the first end of the lace. Conceal these whippings as much as possible by never crossing a hole and keep them all about the same depth, especially in the net.

For (*b*) take the foot pr right through the lace in wh st to the head, tie a reef knot with the outside head pr. Then pick up the bobbins in prs and tie off with reef knots, using each pr as one thread. Cut off leaving several inches if the use is undecided or neatly close to the knot if going to be sewn in. If there is a cluster of threads, such as at the point of a leaf, as in Honiton or similar shapes, move all the middle prs to one side over an outside pr. With this pr and the pr on the other side make a wh st. Now place all the middle prs on top of this wh st and between the two outside prs, make one wh st with them and tie off with a reef knot. Cut the rest off close but be quite sure that the bunch of threads is firmly held.

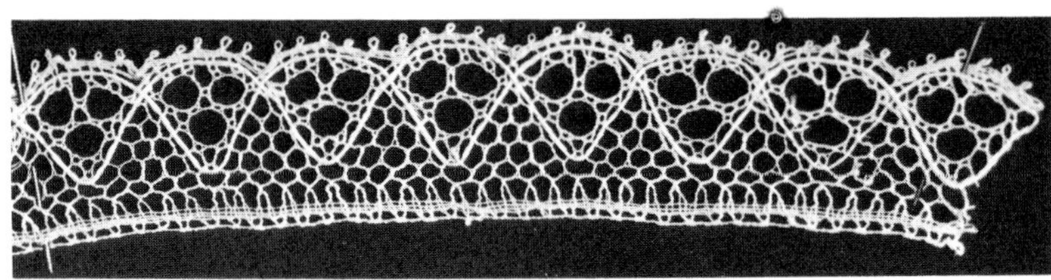

18. Sheep's Head

5. *Sheep's Head*

Abbreviations in this chapter:

wh st	whole stitch
$\frac{1}{2}$ stitch	half stitch
tw	twist
rt pr	right pair
lt pr	left pair
Hc	Honeycomb

Pricking on 10 to the inch. 120 or finer thread.

Bobbin requirements: 14 pairs and 1 gimp pair.

In the next pattern we use the net and foot learnt in the previous exercise plus Honeycomb net, the use of two gimps and the purl pins for the head.

HONEYCOMB NET (illustrations overleaf)

This is worked on the same pricking as net ground except that on the diagonal lines of holes every alternate line has alternate holes left out. The complete line is called the 'long row' and the alternate row the 'short row'.

The stitch is a $\frac{1}{2}$ stitch with only 2 tws, pin up, close round the pin with another $\frac{1}{2}$ stitch with 2 tws. The long row is worked continuously as in net (except for the closing round the pin), then in working back the prs are taken 2 at a time to make a Hc stitch into the available holes, leaving 2 prs hanging from each pin. This gathering together makes the Hc space.

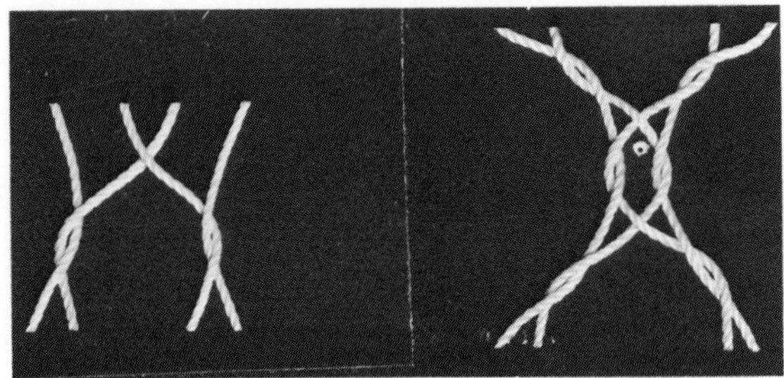

19. Honeycomb Stitch 1 and 2

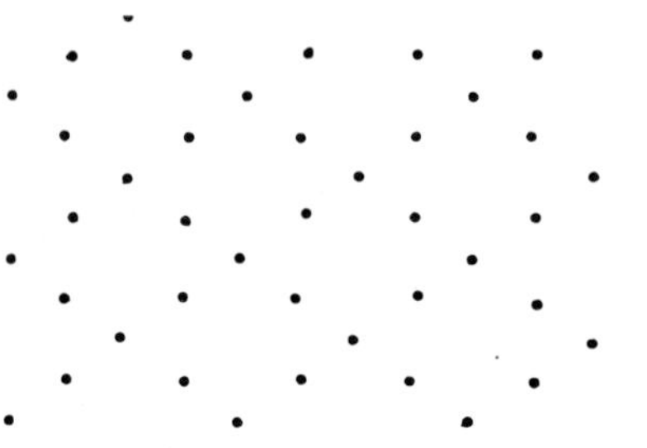

Diagram 11. Honeycomb pricking

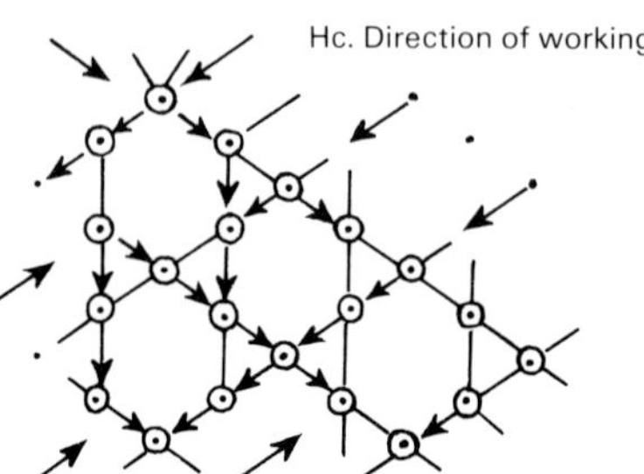

Diagram 12. Honeycomb working

GIMPS

These are worked as the single gimp but are hung on as a pr. Because of the thickness of this thread, wind enough for two on one bobbin and then wind off on to the 2nd so as to avoid a join early in the work. Each gimp travels round the pattern in opposite directions and back to each other where they are *crossed*, i.e. left over right. It is important for the regular appearance of the lace that they should always be crossed not twisted. For taking the gimp through the prs see 'Little Fan', page 30.

THE PURL PIN

This is made by bringing a working pr out from the head, through the gimp weaving wh st through any passives there may be lying there and then:
Twist the workers 5 times. Lift the outside bobbin with the left hand, put a head pin on the thread (Diagram 13), twist it down and up and stick in hole with the thread from the bobbin lying *under* the threads from the lace. Then pick up the right-hand bobbin and twist it round the outside of the head pin and down between the pin and the lace and lay down on the left of the 1st bobbin, the top thread lying above all the twists. These loops should be left very loosely round

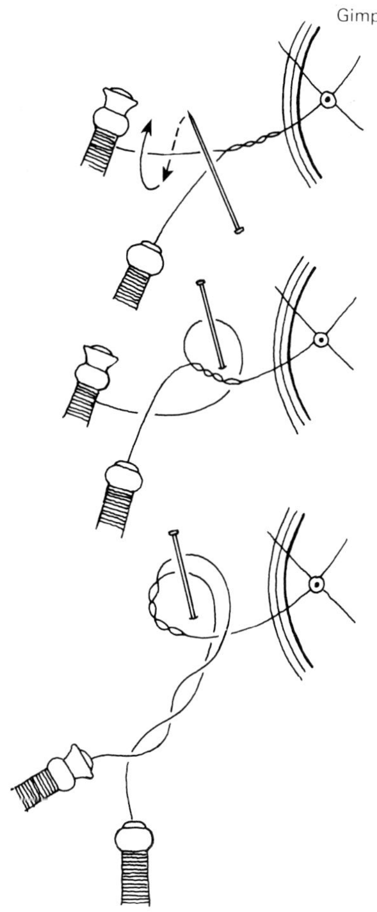

Diagram 13. 'The Purl Pin'

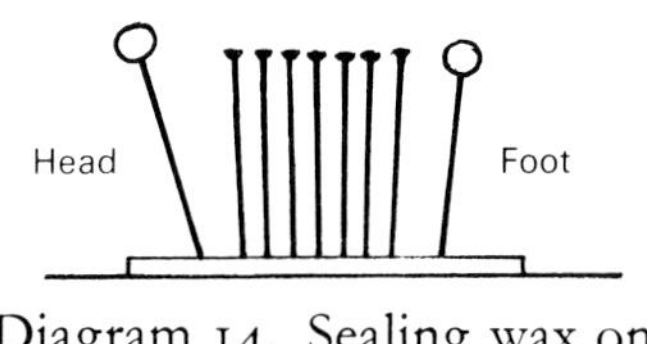

Diagram 14. Sealing wax on head and foot pins

Diagram 15. The pricking for Sheep's Head

the pin during this operation because *now* both bobbins should be carefully tightened so that the five twists lie round the pin. Tw 3 times. If one or the other has been pulled tight before this it would be impossible to have the desirable firmly-twisted purl. 'Split purls' are a very common fault among careless lace makers and tend to lose their identity in washing. It is of assistance to adopt the old custom of putting a blob of sealing wax or a goose grass or similar round hard seed on the top of the head pins as these tend to hold the loose loops down on the pin during the operation. The old workers used to develop this craft need into elaborate decorations of beads and seeds but a simple blob is all that is required. It is a help to treat the foot pins in the same manner but using a different colour of wax. See Diagram 14.

When sticking the head pins and, to a lesser extent, the foot pins, lean them very slightly outwards from the lace. This helps to hold the tension firm and enables a better watch to be kept on what you are doing in these important areas.

THE PRICKING

Note when copying the pricking that the outer Hc rings have been slightly distorted to give a rounder effect to the head. To demonstrate this in the working diagram (Diagram 16) the first head (*a*) has been drawn strictly and the second (*b*) adjusted to get the effect required. This little trick is usually done but only at the head side, not in inside shapes to any great extent.

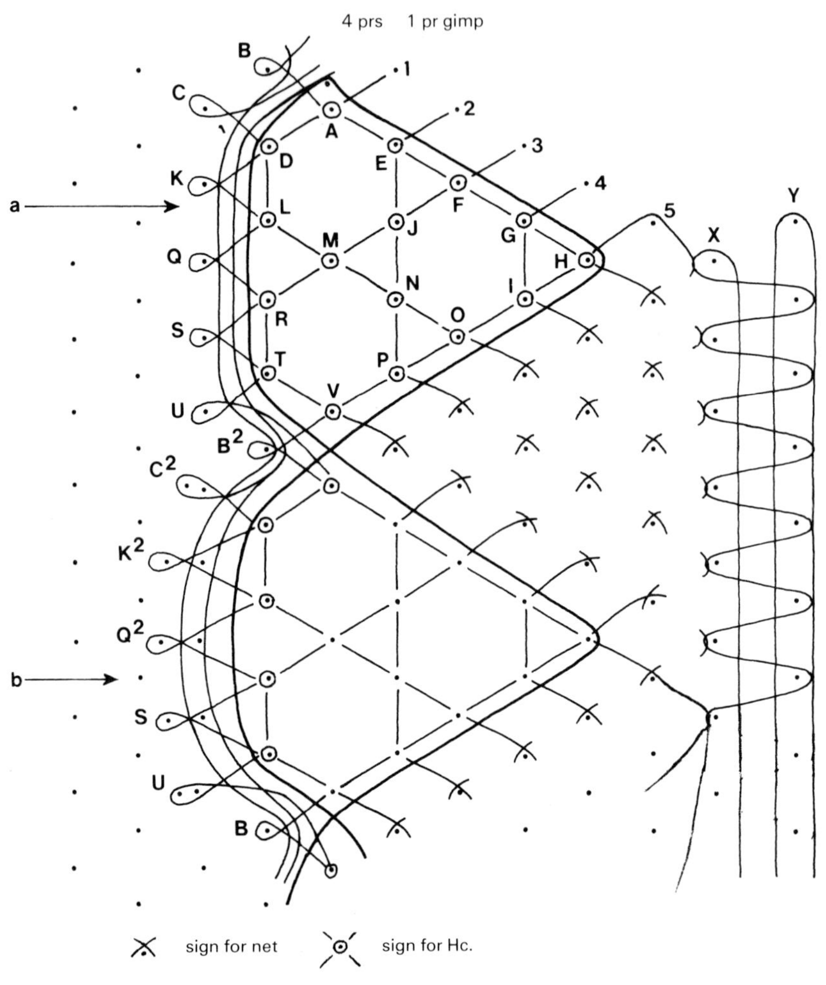

Diagram 16. Setting up for Sheep's Head

THE LACE: SETTING UP (*Diagram* 16)

At the pin hole above A hang on 4 prs and a pr of gimps, leaving all 4 prs lying to left and gimp prs to right of pin. With the left-most pr weave through 3 prs to the right, pass 1 gimp. Tw 2 and leave. With 2 outside prs make purl pin at B. With same 2 prs make purl at C and weave through to gimp, pass and tw 2. Hang pair from a temporary pin at 1, pass through right-hand gimp. It will be found helpful to hitch this gimp temporarily on a pin at the foot until the line of honeycomb stitches inside the head are worked. With the 1st pr in the head and the pr from 1 make a honeycomb stitch (Hc) at A. With the left-hand pr from A and the pr from C make Hc at D. Move these to the left and make Hc at E with the right-hand from A and a new pr, coming through the gimp, from 2. With rt pr from E and a new pr from 3 make Hc F, repeating this at G and H with a new pr from 4 and the lt of 2 prs at 5. With the rt pr from H go through the unhitched gimp, twisting twice after doing so. With lt pr from H and the pr hanging from G make Hc at I, taking rt pr through gimp. Moving up to J make Hc with the prs hanging from E and F. Going to the head side, with the lt pr from D go through the gimp, tw 2, wh st through the passives, purl at K, weave back through passives and gimp, tw 2, make Hc at L with the pr hanging from D. With the rt pr from L and the lt pr from J make Hc at M. With rt pr from M and pr from J make Hc N.

With rt pr from N and lt pr from I make Hc O. Take rt pr through gimp. With lt pr from N and rt pr from O make Hc P. Take rt pr through gimp. Return to head side with lt pr from L, go through gimp and passives to make purl Q, weave back to make Hc R, with lt pr from M. With lt pr from R weave back and make purl pin S and weave back to make Hc st with rt pr from R at T. Weave out and make purl U and leave prs on outside.

With rt pr from T and lt pr from P make Hc V. Take rt pr through rt gimp and lt pr through lt gimp, *cross the gimps*, tw pairs 2, take up 1st passive outside gimp, tw twice, make wh st with pr from V. Tw both twice, weave lt and purl at B2. It is possible in this pattern to take the pr from this purl into the next head to make Hc A, but the passive prs at this corner do tend to climb the pin at B, so if you find yourself in this difficulty use the passive pr running nearest the gimp to do this stitch when you come to it, leaving the prs at B after doing wh st after the purl. In this pricking it is possible to make the purl at B, but often, if this angle is deeper, it is quite correct to make a wh st Hc, i.e. wh st, pin up, close with wh st at this corner.

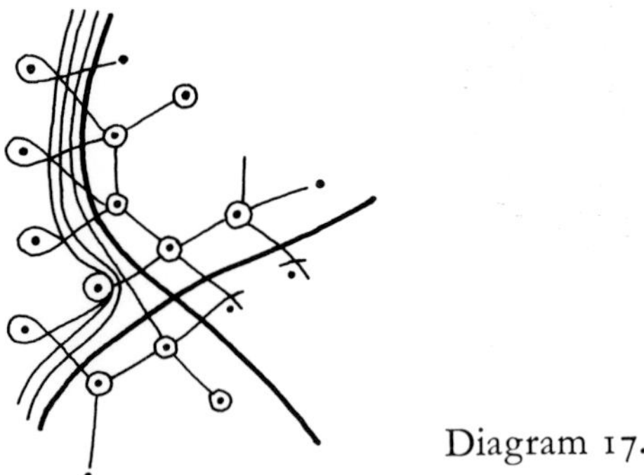

Diagram 17.

Take up two outside prs at head, make wh st, purl pin at B2, weave back, pass gimp, tw 2 and leave.

Repeat at C2, through gimp, tw 2 and leave. Comb all bobbins over to the lt. Hang two prs on catch pin at X and 2 prs on foot pin at Y, remembering to match the two passive prs of bobbins as in 'Little Fan'. With pr from 5 and left-hand pr from X make catch-pin stitch and with prs coming through the gimp from H, I, O, P, V, continue down the line of net stitches, pinning up as you go. When the pr from V has been used, pass the lt pr to the lt through the gimp, making sure the gimps have been *crossed*.

Return to the two catch-pin prs as in 'Little Fan', work rt pr to foot and back, catch pin, catch-pin stitch and the net stitches to the gimp, as before and repeat until the last net stitch is made. Work the next foot and catch-pin stitch and leave. Move bobbins and right gimp over to right of pillow and commence the Hc head as previously done, remembering the last pr coming in from the net to make the Hc at the point must immediately go out through the gimp to make the first net stitch.

After two or three foot crossings have been made it is advisable to release the pins at X and Y on which the four foot prs were hung and very gently pull the passives to get rid of the loops that may be left there.

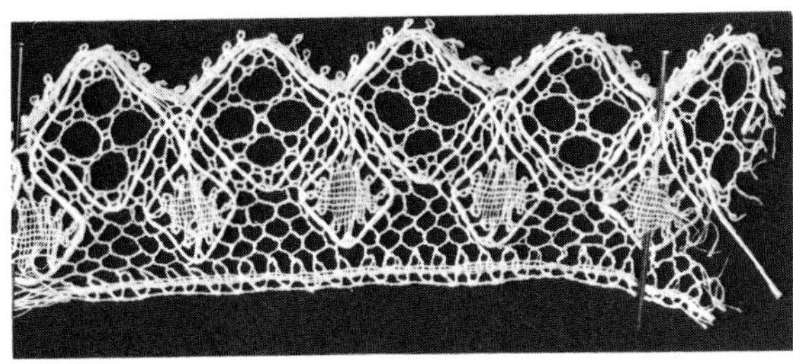

20. Duke's Garter

6. Duke's Garter

Abbreviations as in previous patterns.
Bobbin requirements 20 prs, 1 gimp pair. 120–150 thread.

SETTING UP (see diagrams overleaf)

On pin at A hang a pr of gimps and take to the right. On the same pin hang 6 prs, leaving 5 to the left of the gimp, taking the 6th, that on the furthest right, through the gimp.

On B hang 2 prs, make wh st round pin, take lt pr through gimp and make a wh st with the pr which came through the other gimp. (This stitch and those at B, C, D, E will be Hc stitches in the lace at subsequent heads.)

Take rt pr from B through gimp.

Hang a single pr round pin in C and take through gimp. Repeat at D and E.

Hang 2 prs on pin at F and G, H and I. Take lt pr from F through gimp to left.

With rt pr from F and lt pr from G make net stitch at J. With rt pr from G and left from H make the catch-pin stitch, i.e. a net stitch with no pin between the prs. With rt pr from J and lt pr from catch pin make net at K.

With rt pr of the catch-pin prs weave through foot passives, wh st to rt, tw 3 times, tw the outside pr 3 times, make wh st with worker, put pin up under both at L, weave wh st through foot passives, tw worker 3 times, put up catch pin at M and do catch-pin stitch.

Take the prs from F, J, K and the lt pr from catch pin M through gimp to the left. You are now ready to do the *cloth work 'bud'*, with 8 prs hanging within the gimp all twisted twice.

Diagram 18. Duke's Garter

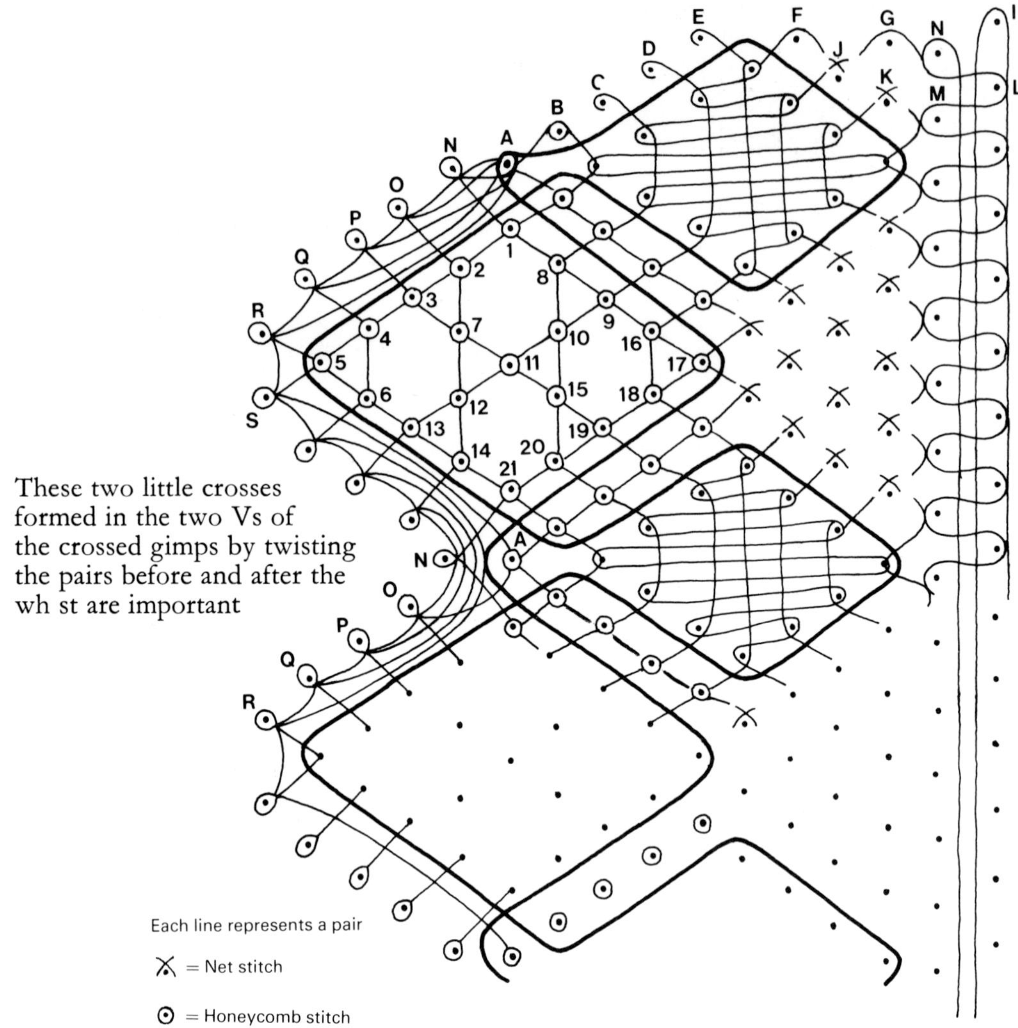

With the two highest, middle prs, hanging from E and F, make wh st, tw 2 both, stick pin in top hole close round pin with wh st. With lt pr (the workers) make wh st with the pair from D tw workers twice, pin up, close round pin, weave to rt taking in pr from J, tw 2, pin up, close round pin and weave to left.

Repeat this weaving from side to side, taking in the pr each time, twisting the *workers only* twice before sticking pin under them, until the outer points of the bud have been worked when, on the diminishing sides a pr will be left out at each of the pin holes on each side. When weaving of the bud is completed the gimp is

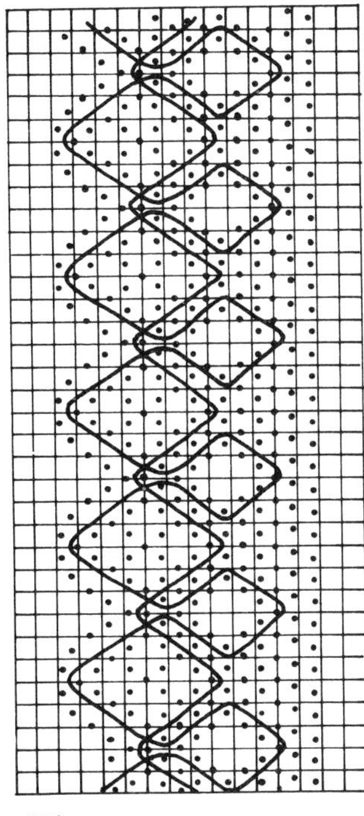

Diagram 19.

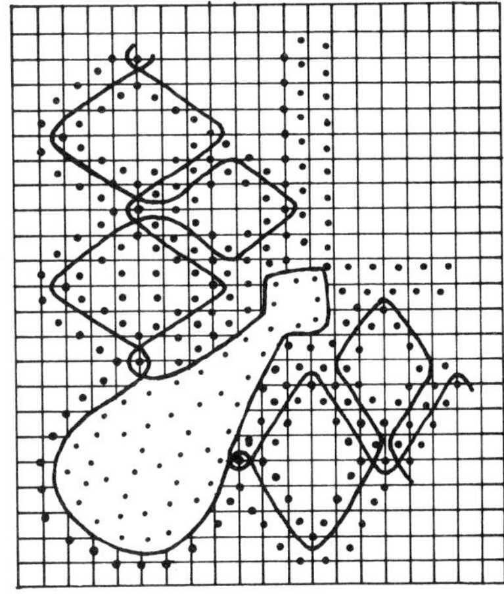

Diagram 20.
Pricking for Duke's Garter

brought through all 8 prs from the foot side down four, which will make net, up four towards the centre. It is then passed through the rt pr from A and crossed with the other gimp.

With rt pr from A and the pr from the bud make Hc sts in the 4 holes lying below the bud, and taking the lt-hd prs through the new gimp. Move all these well over to the left of the pillow returning to the rt catch-pin pr at M.

Work through the foot, back, catch pin and stitch, and 4 net stitches, taking in for the last the rt pr from the last Hc. Take lt pr through gimp making 5 prs hanging through the gimp inside the Hc bud. As it is not possible to complete the net block until the lt-hd pr from this pin comes out again, move all bobbins over to the right.

With the two outside pairs hanging from A make a purl pin at N. Weave rt pr through passives tw 2 before and after making wh st with pr from A, take through gimp.

Weave pr from A left to purl O, back through passives and through gimp. Push bobbins to R. With two outside prs make purl pin P, weave to gimp and through.

Repeat this at Q and R by which time all the passives will have been used and there are 5 prs hanging, twisted through the gimp.

We now work the Hc 'bud'. Spread out the bobbins to open up the space and with the pr from N and the pr from the top Hc in the run of 4 work Hc stitch at 1. With lt pr from 1 and pr from O work Hc at 2 and so on down the long row to 5. Take lt pr from 5 through gimp to left, through to purl at S and leave. For the short row take rt pr from 5 and pr from 4, Hc st 6, leave. Take prs from 3 and 2 Hc st at 7, leave. Take pr from 1 and next pr on right, Hc st at 8. With rt pr from 8 and new pr Hc st at 9. Then work the 'long' line 10, 11, 12, 13 with the prs in order from 8, 7 and 6, taking the last on the left each time through the gimp and the passives, making the purl and leaving. Work back through Hc 'short' line at 14, 15 and 16. Work the long line, Hc st at 17, 18, 19, 20 and 21 with the prs, in order, from 16, 15 and 14, taking the rt prs through the gimp to the R and the lt pr, to the left at 21, cross the gimps, and weave lt pr to the left through the gimp and passives to purl at N weaving back to the last passive, tw 2.

Now return to the net block, passing the bobbins to the left till you come to the 2 catch-pin prs. With the rt pr work foot and back, then 4 net stitches using the pr from the point of. the Hc bud for the last one. Work 4 Hc sts down the line of the gimp. Move the bobbins back to the left bringing the right gimp through all the pairs from the 4 Hc sts only and leave. Move up to foot, work foot, catch pin and 3 nets; foot, catch pin and 2 nets; foot, catch pin and 1 net; foot and catch pin, passing the 4 lt prs through the gimp at the end of each net line ready for the wh st bud. Work the wh st bud.

With the innermost passive pr next to the outside gimp round the Hc Head, tw 2, pass gimp, tw 2 and make Hc at A with the bottom pr from the upper line of 4 Hc. Now pass gimp from foot side of wh st bud down through the prs on the right, which will go in to the net and up the lt side and the rt pr from A. Make the lower line of four Hc st beginning with the rt pr from A and the lt pr from the corner of the wh st bud. Move all these bobbins over to the right. Take lt pr from A, through gimp, through pr from N, tw 2, wh st through all passives to purl at O and back to the gimp, tw 2. The purls at P, Q and R are now worked, each using the two outside prs, and weaving back through the passives and leaving the worker twisted twice. The 2 gimps are now crossed, the lt hd taken through the 5 twisted prs from the purls, the right through the 4 prs, the 5th coming in when the 1st line of net is done, ahead of the net block.

If a wider lace is required prick the head part of the pattern down to the point of the cloth work diamond, which is on an intersecting line of the graph paper. Move the tracing to the left 3 squares, i.e. to the place where the next spot on the intersecting line comes. Then prick the extra lines of net and the 2 foot rows.

Having mastered this pattern there are one or two helpful short cuts that a practised lacemaker may take.

When making the net – after putting up the catch pin – it is quicker to make all the line of net stitches down to the gimp and *then* pin up while moving the bobbins over to the left to the foot, taking great care that you put the pins between the right prs, i.e. 1 pr between each pin with prs coming out at 52°, and make sure that there are 2 prs at the catch-pin stitch, i.e. hung between the last 2 pins before the foot.

This method does ensure a more even tension for the net as, if the prs have all been twisted correctly, at the end of the line the left-most bobbin of the last pr has gone straight through from the catch pin and, by holding this pr, especially that bobbin, quite firmly while putting in the pins the net will be in a correct, straight, diagonal line. When making the next line of stitches be even more sure than usual to leave yourself enough room to move the bobbins over in the opposite direction to this line as this settles in the stitches on the other diagonal and makes the pinning easier.

7. *Floral Patterns, etc.*

Tallies. Hc Rings. Mayflower. Additional Gimps. Stems. Kat Stitch Ground. Flowers with Holes. Setting Up. Examples of Errors.

FLORAL PATTERNS

See Appendix B on *The Pricking* under 'Buds and Heads'. Having done the 'Duke's Garter' these patterns can be understood or worked out, the chief points to remember being that the cloth work must be woven straight across. If the curve of a shape has caused the weaving line to begin to slope, prevent this by repeating a pin hole in this way. Weave to the offending side, close round pin but do not take out the last passive. With the inner of the pin prs weave to the next hole the other side and back where another edge stitch is made in the same hole and then the outgoing pr is taken out at its proper place. Or sometimes a *Turning Stitch* is used instead of this double use of the edge hole on the inside of the curve. This is done by working a wh st and a ½ st with the last 2 prs, leave the outside pr and weave back with the inner.

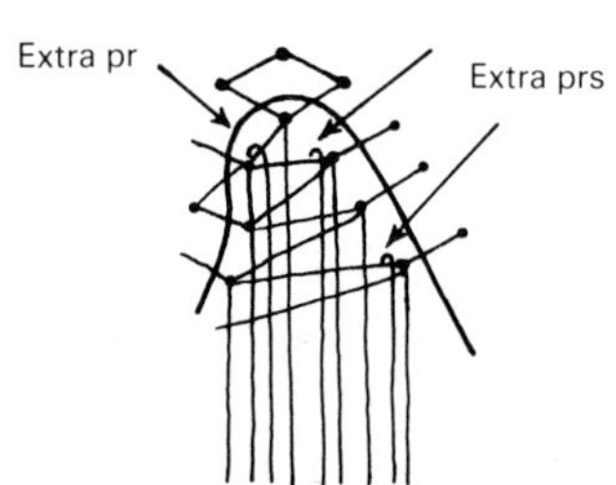

Diagram 21*a*.

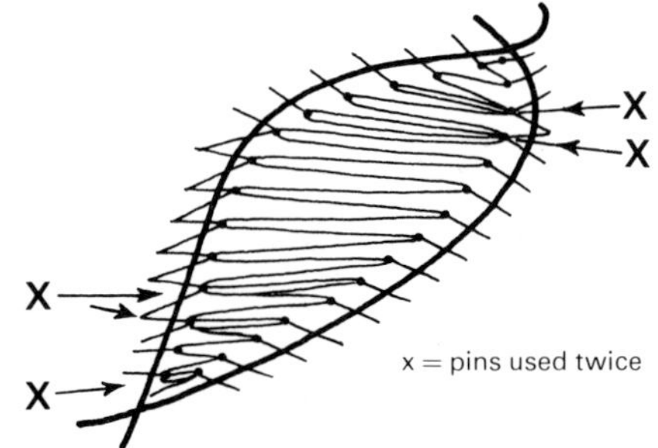

Diagram 21*b*.

There must always be the right number of prs coming out of a shape to make the net – no less and no more. Any extra prs needed to thicken up the cloth work of a leaf or flower must be hung on to the workers before working the edge hole with them and then at the end be carried out and on with the gimps or taken out in the narrowing end of the leaf where the weaving is tight. It is inadvisable to hang any extra prs in sprigs that are separately dotted about in the net.

To take out extra prs no longer required just lift them one at a time back over the lace to hang down at the back of the pillow. When the lace has moved on a few rows these can be cut off leaving a few inches of thread and rejoined in prs for future use. The ends left can usually be cut off close to the work without detriment. If, however, they come in a loose part, thread on to a short needle and whip or darn in.

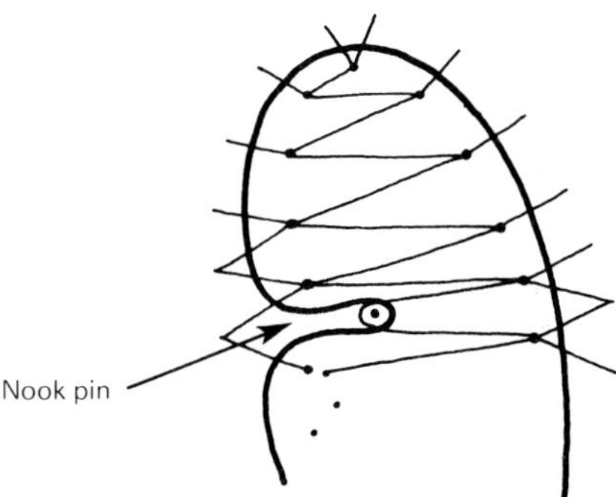

Diagram 22. Nook pins

Nook pins. These indentations in leaves using the gimp thread must be very securely anchored at the turn of the nook by the weaver – or a pr from the other side used as a weaver – coming through the gimp tw 3, stick pin under and return through gimp to further pin hole. Do *not* make a pin hole with 2 prs and then weave on.

TALLIES (*see diagrams overleaf*)

These are square dots found in many laces. They are sometimes called 'lead work', plaits or cut work but these terms are apt to confuse. They are found in *point net* where they are marked in the pricking by an ink dot instead of a pin hole and are made with the 2 prs coming from the 2 parallel holes above the dot.

In *Kat Stitch* they are usually marked in over the place where the whole stitches are made on the way back to the foot.

In *Honeycomb* they are usually made inside a honeycomb ring.

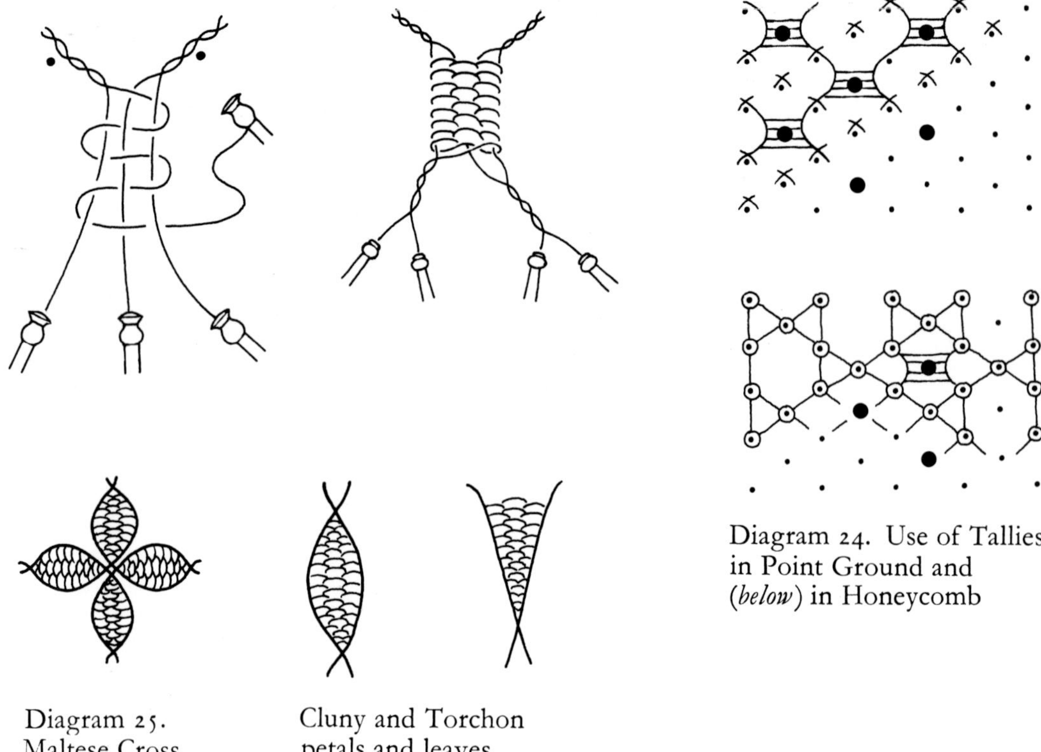

Diagram 24. Use of Tallies in Point Ground and (*below*) in Honeycomb

Diagram 25. Maltese Cross.

Cluny and Torchon petals and leaves

They may appear singly, in groups of various spacings, but it is essential they should be marked by an ink dot as otherwise it is so easy to pass by the space especially when working at speed.

This attractive little spot is made with 2 prs from the ground. The 2nd bobbin from the left is taken up and lengthened. Holding this in the right hand and keeping the outer 2 bobbins well spread with the little fingers of both hands weave over the middle, under and over right, under middle, over and under the left, etc. Pull up the weaver to shape holding the outer bobbins very firm after every 2 or 3 crossings and keep the number of crossings even in any group. The weaver must never be dropped but always held with a loose thread except when pulling up, but even then the weaving should have been made at such a tension that the pulling up should be done by the widening of the prs on the pillow rather than any pulling of the weaver. The aim in the spot is to have it square.

In Torchon and other laces this weaving is controlled in to a variety of shapes to make a Maltese Cross with both ends pulled to a point or with square ends in Beds Maltese, Cluny and Torchon petals and leaves.

In all of these the prs coming in must be twisted at least twice, usually 3 times, and at the end the weaver is wound up to the same length as the passives, tw 3 times with the lt-hd bobbin and the 2 other ones are also tw 3 times. It is advisable to have the lines of ground worked well up to the tallies, or leaves, so that these prs can be worked into it as soon as possible to save accidental misshaping taking place.

HONEYCOMB RINGS

Sometimes singly, sometimes in festoons these are a most useful pattern. They consist of the 6 holes of the honeycomb, surrounded by gimps and need 4 prs coming through the gimp. The 2 middle prs make the top hole and then divide to make the left and right holes with the other 2 prs. The outer prs are then taken

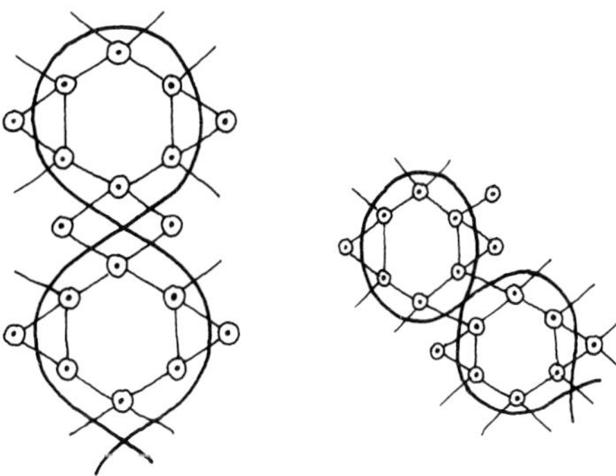

Diagram 26. Honeycomb Rings

out through the gimps to make a purl or net stitch outside the ring and brought back in again where they each Hc with the pairs still inside. The left and right prs are then taken out and the inner 2 close the Honeycomb ring before each going out. The gimps are then *crossed* and the following ring or other parts of the lace made. Look at 'True Lovers' Knot', p. 55. It is essential that the gimps be always crossed, i.e. L over R to give an even chain-like effect. This is a general rule but it is even more important in a chain of rings as they are in such close proximity.

MAYFLOWER

is another attractive pattern based on Honeycomb. On a pricking this is often shown as a + in a honeycomb space. This is found sometimes in the middle only of an area of honeycomb and sometimes in every alternate space. It consists of a large spot of weaving using the prs that would have made the Hc. See 'Plum Pudding' below and the old Bucks sample on page 12.

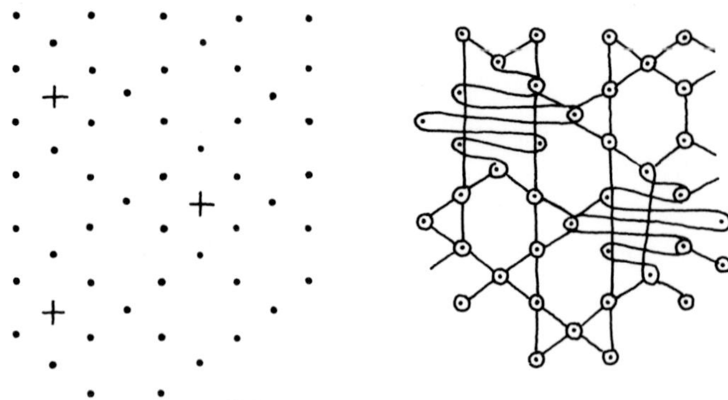

Diagram 27. Mayflower

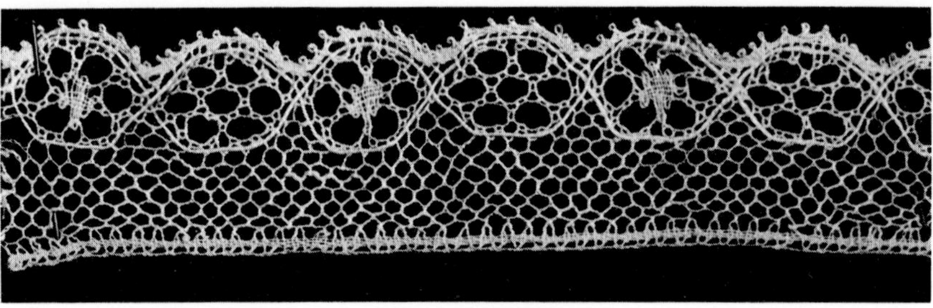

21. Plum Pudding

ADDITIONAL GIMPS

On looking at a complicated pattern try in the first place to see if 1 pr of gimps can be used. A piece of tracing paper placed over the inked pricking is a great help. The old lacemakers very rarely hung on extra ones and took them out but instead carried through double in order to use them elsewhere. This method of double tracking often enables one to use only 1 pr instead of 2 – or even more. Care must be taken to see that where they do lie double they lie flat and evenly alongside each other. A gimp, to be effective, should be considerably thicker than the lace thread and therefore would look clumsy twisted. If, however, 2 thin threads are being used as a gimp, these may sometimes with advantage be twisted. If a broader flat line is required such as running along the bottom side of a leaf then this can be obtained by passing 1 gimp through the pr and giving 1 tw before passing the other through. These gimps are usually going in opposite directions so this is quite easy to do. Extra care is needed in ensuring that there are twists before and after the gimps when they are going through double.

There are no different problems when an extra pair has to be used beyond planning the routes taken and ensuring that they are used in a regular way and not different in each head. It may prove helpful to mark the 2nd gimp line of the pr in a coloured ink – but be sure it is not smudgable.

When a *sprig* or dot appears in the net and a gimp is required round it the gimp bobbins at the finish must be crossed and run double through 2 or 3 prs at least and then taken back over the pillow. The weight of the bobbins lying back will help to firm the gimp round the sprig and the twisting of the prs will hold them firm. Do not cut off until required for further sprigs and leave enough end to hold when the final cutting is done.

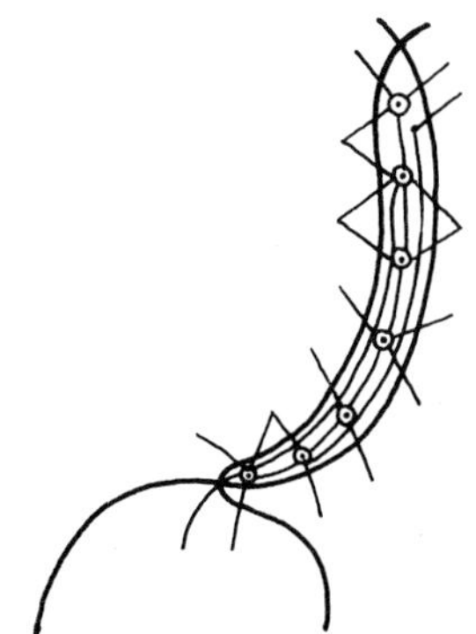

Diagram 28. Stems

STEMS

A gimp or even double gimps wandering through the net are weak in appearance. The best method is to work them with a gimp each side of a row of honeycomb holes. These stems are often used as convenient trunk roads to carry extra prs from one part of the lace to another. The centre pin holes are made at convenient places to bring prs in from the net to make the honeycomb stitches, 1 pr being retained to run down the middle of the stem – extra prs are brought through the gimps and carried between them and the centre holes.

KAT STITCH, WIRE OR FRENCH GROUND (*see diagram overleaf*)

This is an alternative to the point ground but is pricked slightly differently. See Appendix B on 'Pricking', page 103. It requires 4 prs per pin hole for the net and the same as point for the foot., i.e. 2 passives and a foot pr but in the foot the worker and the passives are twisted once between each wh st as in Torchon. For the net which is worked diagonally in wh st with 1 tw after each crossing, other prs will be hung on with 2 prs between each pin hole commencing at *a*. After working through the foot passives make a wh st with twist with the next net pr,

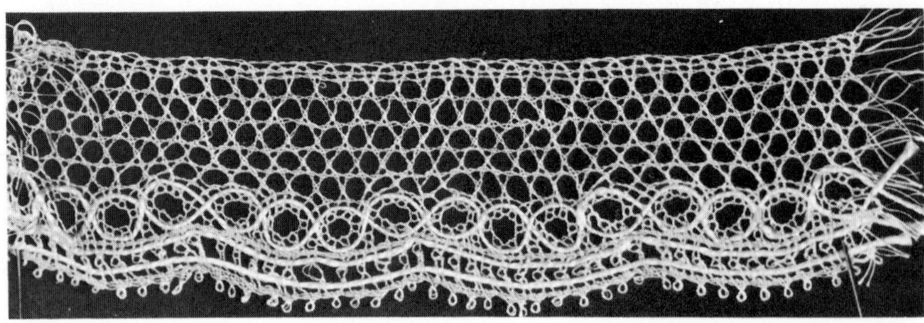

22. Kat stitch edging

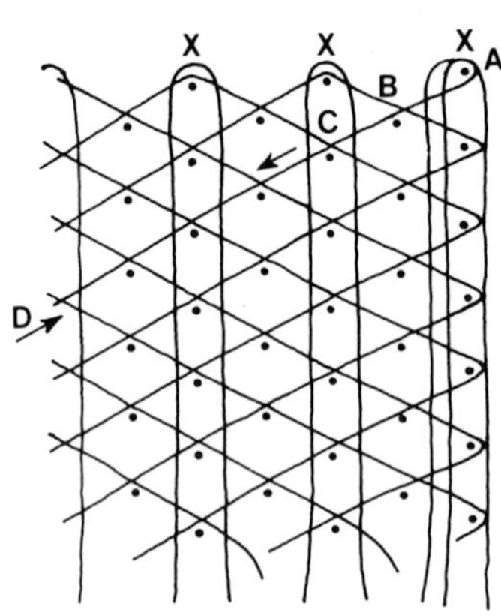

Diagram 29. Kat Stitch.
Hang 2 prs of pairs at each X.
Each line represents a pair
and each crossing is wh st.

pin *b* between but do not close, make wh st with 1 tw, another wh st with 1 tw, put up pin *c* and repeat to the gimp or edge of filling. Work back to foot by making wh st with 1 tw with each of the 2 prs hanging between the pins as in the 'short' line of honeycomb *d*. It will be seen that the net consists of a diagonal pair going each way and straight lines dropping down each side of the pin holes. This shape of net must be well understood and care taken when going into and out of the head that enough prs are left out to work the net in the proper way, i.e. that the diagonal and perpendicular prs lie in their right places. This net can be worked by making a ½ stitch at the pin and closing round the pin with another ½ stitch plus 1 tw but this tends to upset the rhythm and therefore the tension of the work.

There follow various prickings and photos of edgings that are worth doing for various reasons and purposes.

In *Flowers* with *holes in the middle*, as in the two prickings (Diag. 34), from Aylesbury Museum, the middle holes are worked as snatch pins. When the top pin hole in the middle has been reached the weaver works to the middle wh st, twist both prs, put up pin and close round it, then with the lt pr weave backwards and forwards to edge and back to middle, twisting 3 times round the pins in the middle. Repeat at the right side. At the bottom of the hole the weavers meet in the middle with a wh st round the pin, 1 pr is left lying straight down and the other goes out to the edge and continues the weaving.

The lace shown in Photo 23 was done by a comparative beginner who had done only a few edgings before attempting them. Mistakes can be seen but a lot can be learnt from them.

In setting up Floral Patterns do not bother to get yourself a set number of bobbins. Just go on hanging on pairs as required, never starving the cloth work. Pairs can always be taken out if found to be unnecessary and a few extra pairs are always found to be useful. Endeavour to get a regular appearance by using the same number of pairs in each head when you have found out what is needed. Numbers have been suggested against some of the prickings but different workers may find they need more or less.

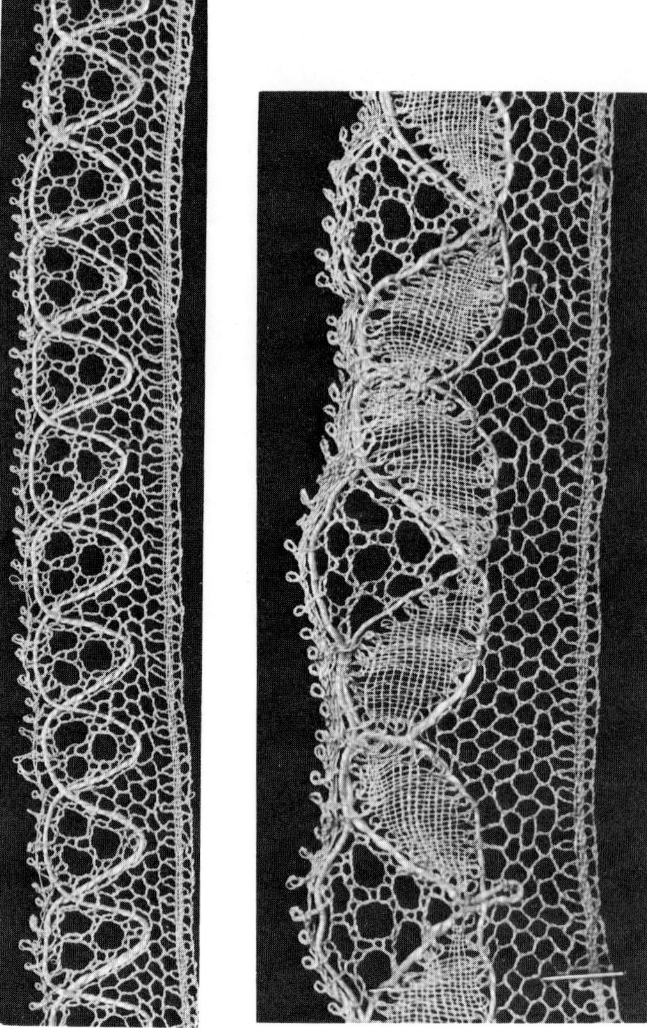

23. Errors

ERRORS

Two examples of beginner's work with valuable lessons to teach.

1: The foot of 'Sheep's Head' was not worked in the correct order resulting in the *catch pin* never looking even. This worker used to leave the foot weaver hanging over the catch pin and did not do the catch-pin stitch until making the net. Therefore always work out from a made catch pin to the foot, back through the foot, catch pin, catch-pin stitch, and down the diagonal line of the net.

2: The Head of 'Sheep's Head' is thin and weak. It needs at least one more passive pair between the purl and the gimp.

3: The purls are frequently split as the first thread has been pulled tight round the pin before the other one has been looped round it.

4: In the enlarged pattern the worker in the woven petal has not always been kept going straight across and the correction has had to be done twice leading to a thickening of the cloth.

5: On the purl side the pupil has not understood the manner in which the purl workers should keep the angle of entry the same as in net. The last two heads are better managed in this respect.

6: In the lower wh st petal of the top head more passives should have been taken into the petal instead of being left outside the gimp. This is better managed in the second head but the innermost passive should have been taken into the lower petal, the top petal of the last head and also at the top of the Honeycomb.

7: *Net.* Enlargement has emphasized some unevenness. It looks much better in reality. The worst fault (which was eventually corrected) is that going into the head at the top of the top petal a stitch should have been made, even if a pin hole is not there, between the 2nd and 3rd prs coming in and again between the 4th and 5th and the 5th and 6th. This group has been better worked on the 3rd head, but where the pin holes are in a straight line downwards inside the petal there should have been an adjacent line outside the petal for the net pr to go into the head, come out to the net to make a net stitch and go back in again. This could have been a fault in an old pricking – it is well to watch for and correct such faults. Note also a knot in the net. This is better avoided.

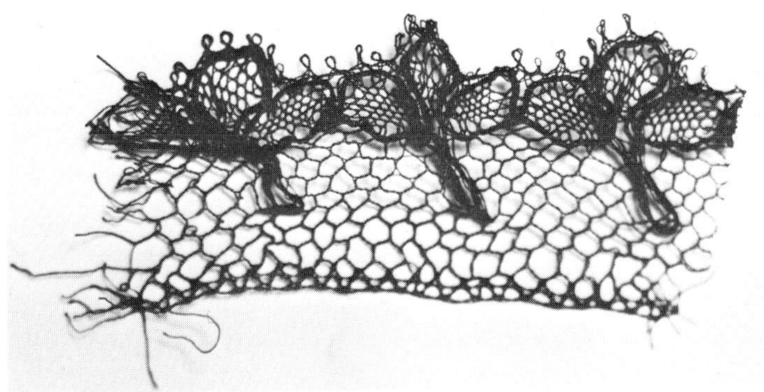

24. True Lovers' Knot, an antique ½ st variant. See Diagram 31

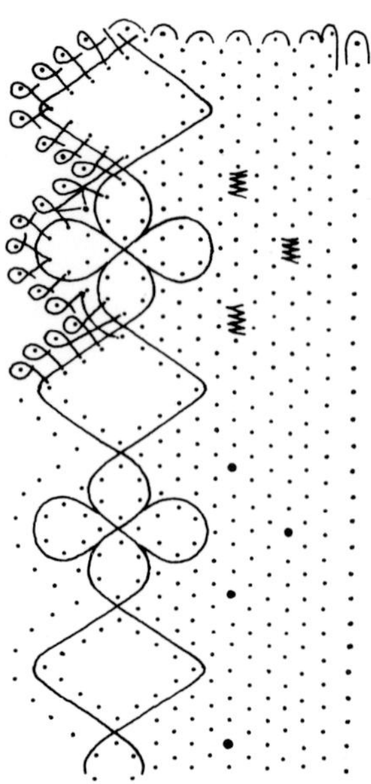

Note. Hc stitch at the junction of rings on head side. Tallies are drawn in on 1st head and indicated in the usual way by a *spot* subsequently. There is no pin hole. 21 prs thread. 1 pr gimps

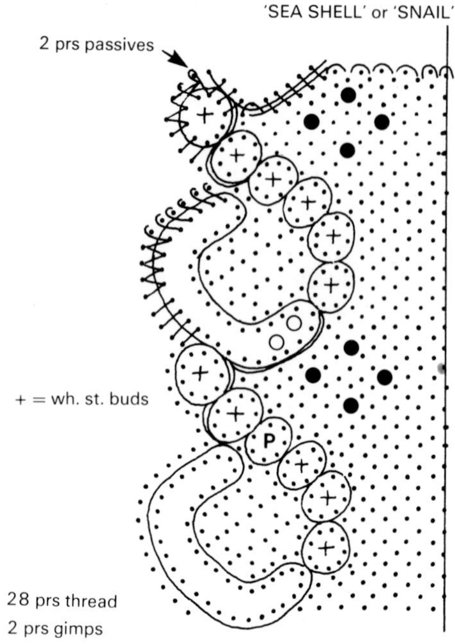

Either take gimps out at o and o, hanging on again at p, *or* carry gimps through at double lines.

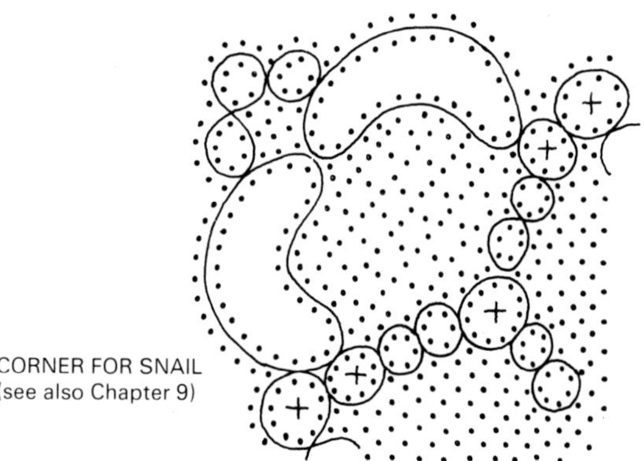

CORNER FOR SNAIL
(see also Chapter 9)

Diagram 30. Various Point patterns

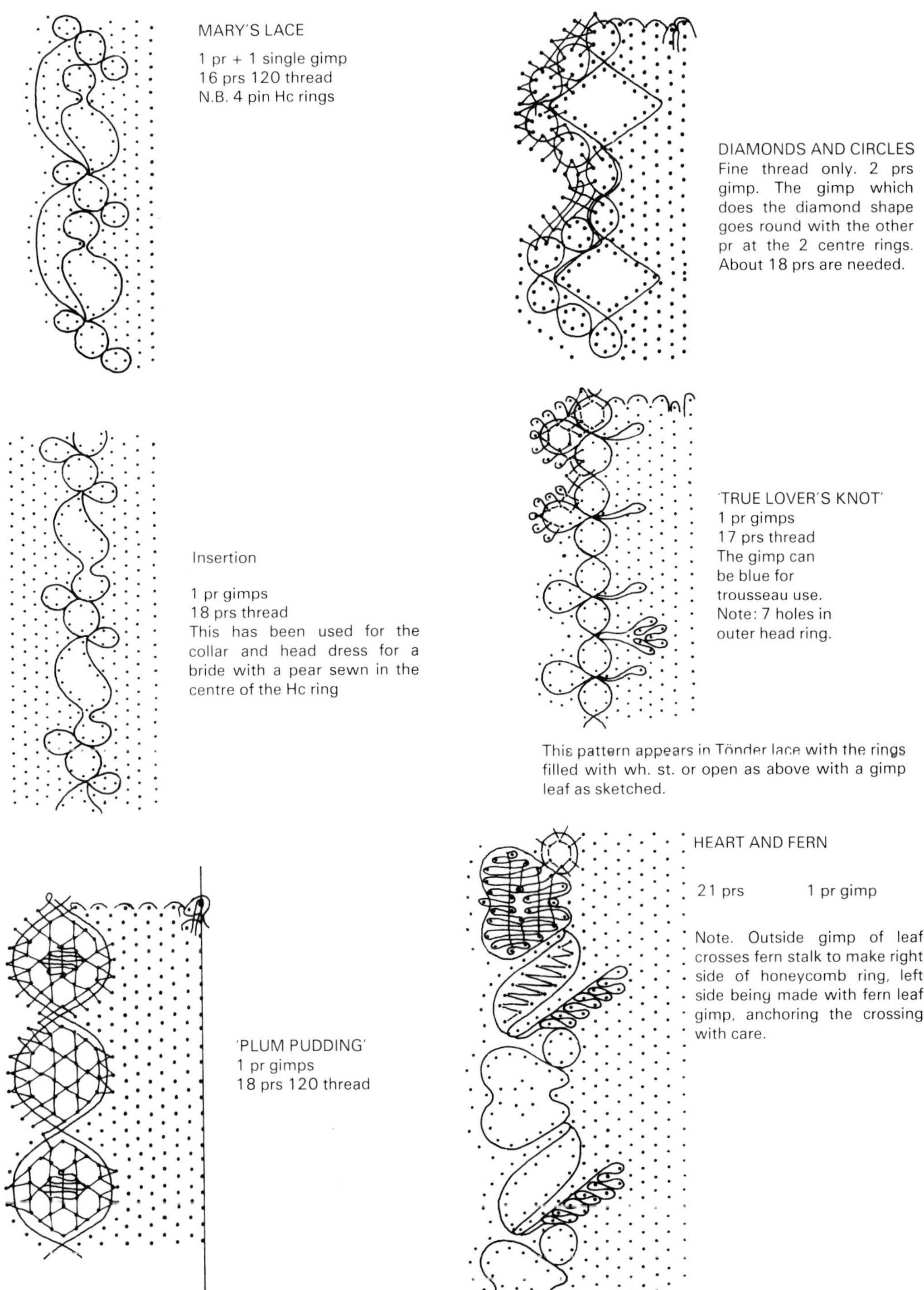

Diagram 31. See also Photo 24 for True Lovers' Knot

25

1 'Strawberry'
19–20 prs. 3 gimps
Note: 1 Nook pin on Head side.
2 An extra pair is carried through the centre to fill the leaves

2 'Little Bean'
15–16 prs. 1 pr gimps

3 Traditionally this pattern is done in black thread, often with half stitch leaves. It was done as shown as an experiment.
Note: crossing of gimps and cutting off at spots

4 Sometimes called 'Rosy Wreath'
Note: 4 pin Honeycomb rings

5 'Cat Face'
Note: The 4 pin 'ears' are done in whole stitch not Hc as in No. 4

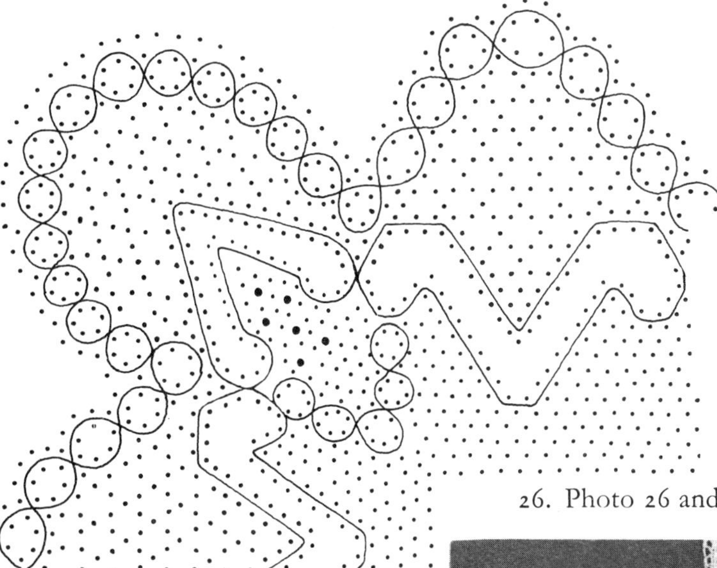

26. Photo 26 and Diagram 32: after Maidment

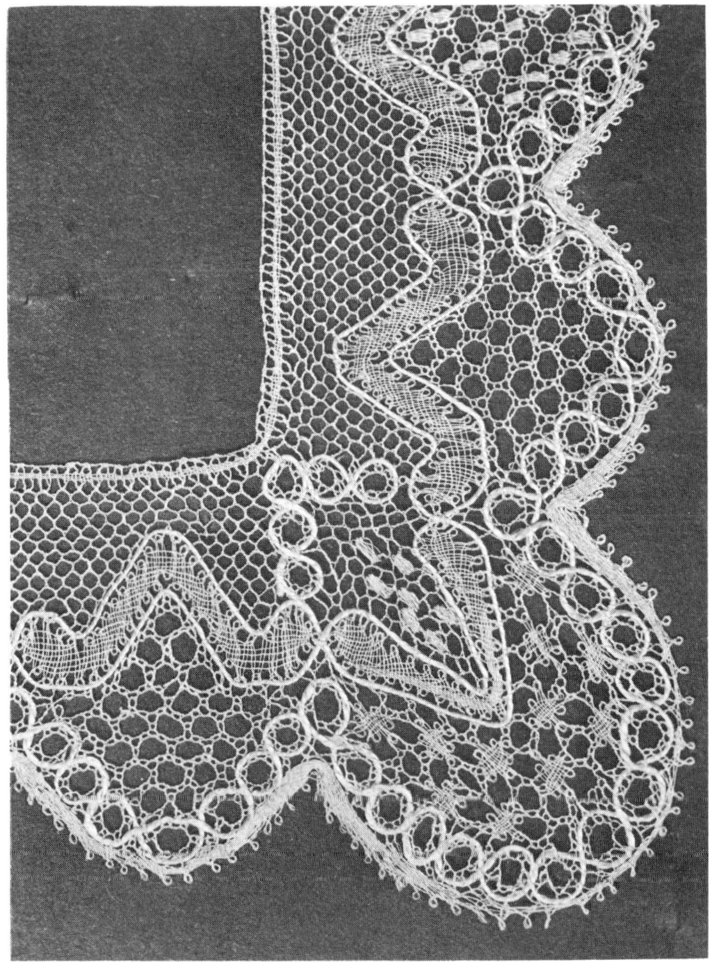

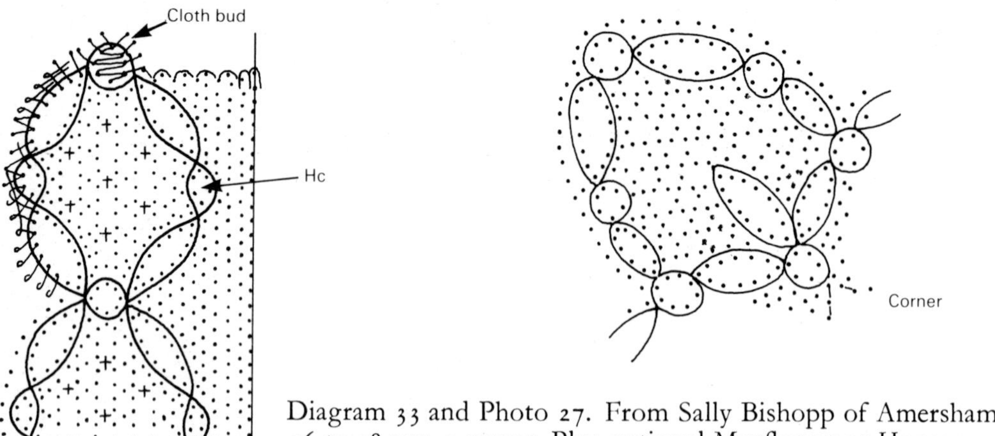

Diagram 33 and Photo 27. From Sally Bishopp of Amersham. 26 to 28 prs. 2 gimps. Plus optional Mayflower or Honeycomb.

28. Point Ground pillow lace. *Luton Museum*

Diagram 34. Two beautiful prickings from the Aylesbury (Bucks) Museum

These were probably originally pricked on millimetre graph paper using a 2 mm sq. so that the drop is 2 mm, the horizontal 3 mm.

Note 1. The centre of the six-petalled flowers, the little circles in *a* and the big petals of *b* are holes of snatch pins.

Note 2. Where a flowing line has to be maintained the line is held by the gimp but the weavers go through to a hole outside and return after making a stitch.

Note 3. Four pin and 6 pin rings and the extra Hc pin in centre net of Large Flower in *b*.

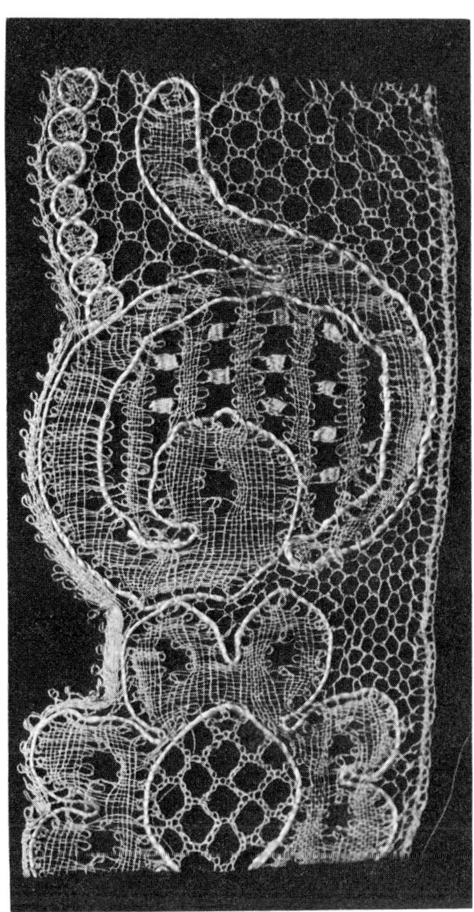

29. Lace from the Aylesbury Museum, prickings opposite

8. *Torchon, Maltese and Cluny*

Torchon lace is a simple lace easily learnt provided 'Point' has been studied first and the tensions and techniques thoroughly mastered. It is a *bad* lace to begin on because the thread used being thicker, with wide spaces to cross between the pin holes, it is tempting sometimes to pick up the bobbins to settle and make firm the twists or plaits. This can be done but tends to lift the loops up the pins which makes the lace uneven. If a student therefore begins on Torchon and takes these bad habits with her to do 'Point', the finer threads will perpetually be breaking and the even tension be almost impossible to get.

THE PRICKING

Torchon is planned on squared paper but all the dots are at line intersections so that the angle of the basic net is at 45°. See Diagram 35*a*. The foot uses the same angles as the net – not as in 'Point'. The curve of the head side is drawn freehand but evenly and the pin holes on it are spaced so as to work in with the net holes opposite to them. If the line of the working pr is drawn in as in (*b*) it can be seen how this is done. Weaving must be kept so that the appearance is parallel as in 'Point'.

The net is worked diagonally and is made with 2 prs per pin hole, a ½ stitch, i.e. cross the middle, twist sides once – pin up, close round with ½ stitch. Between the pin holes 1, 2 or 3 twists can be made according to the distance to be covered and the thickness of the thread used. In the edging shown in Photo 30 in the block of net marked (*a*) 1 twist is used, i.e. ½ stitch, pin, ½ stitch with 1 twist. This gave a light but rather loose effect so the rest of the net was done in ½ stitch, pin, ½ stitch with 2 twists (*b*). Three twists on this pricking would have been too crowded.

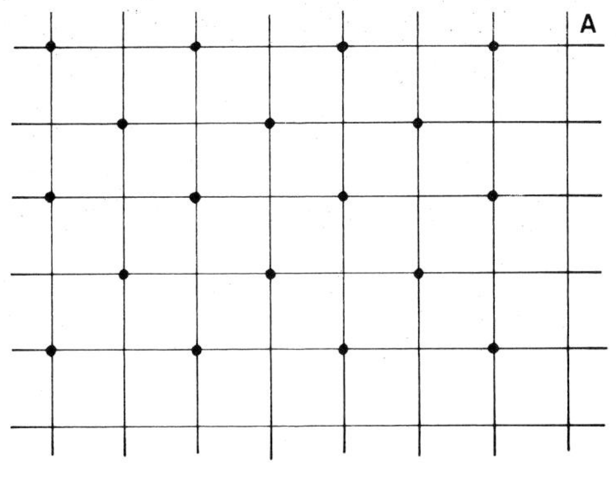

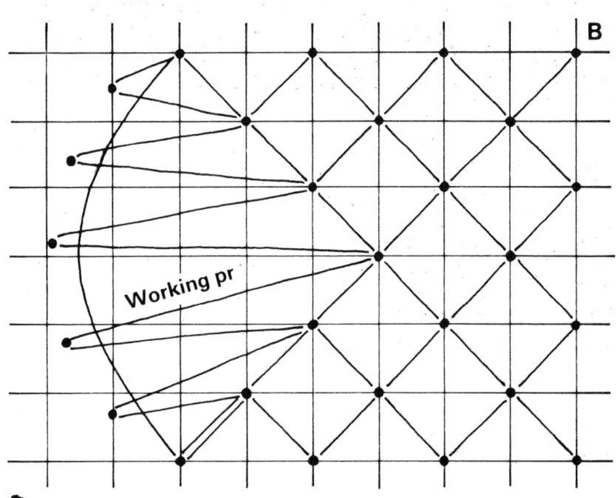

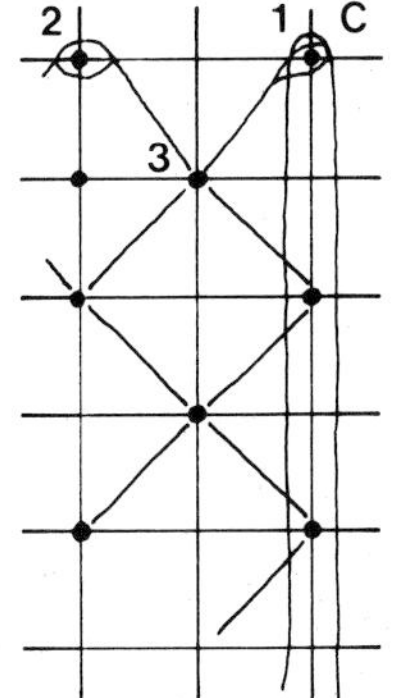

Diagram 35. Torchon pricking

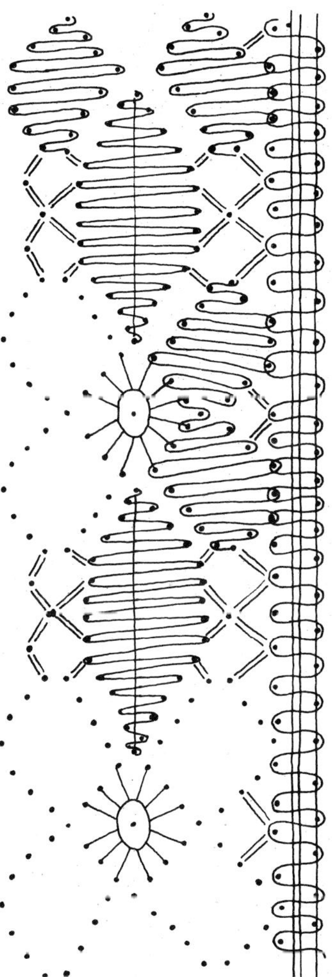

Diagram 36. See photo 31.
38 bobbins. 40 thread. 19 prs

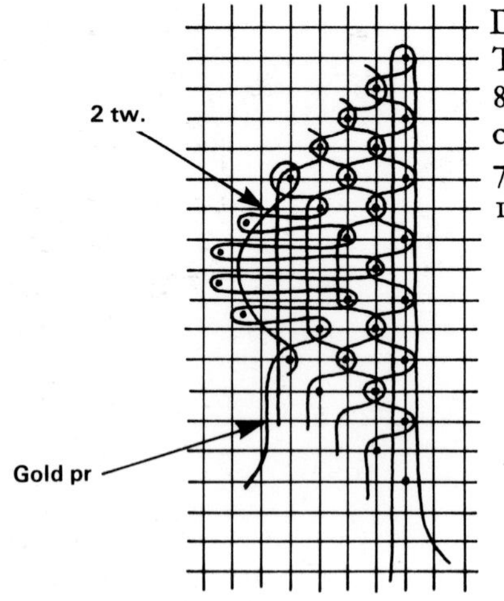

Diagram 37.
Torchon Little Fan.
8 prs
coloured thread or
7 prs thread and
1 pr gold-G.

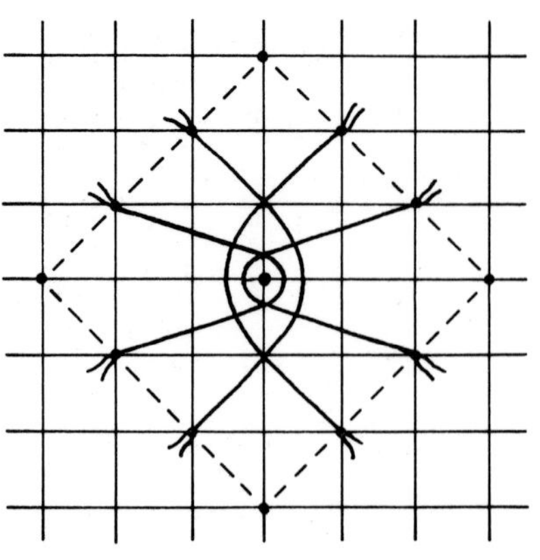

Diagram 38. The Spider

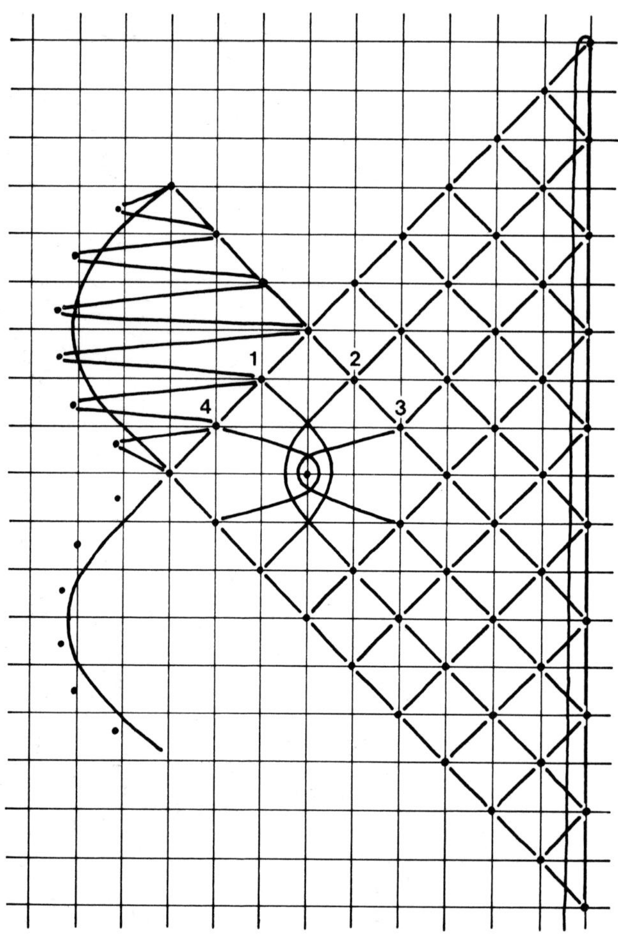

Diagram 39.
Fan and Spider.
Hang on closing round pin and on diagonal.
Keep passives in head moving well to fill fan.

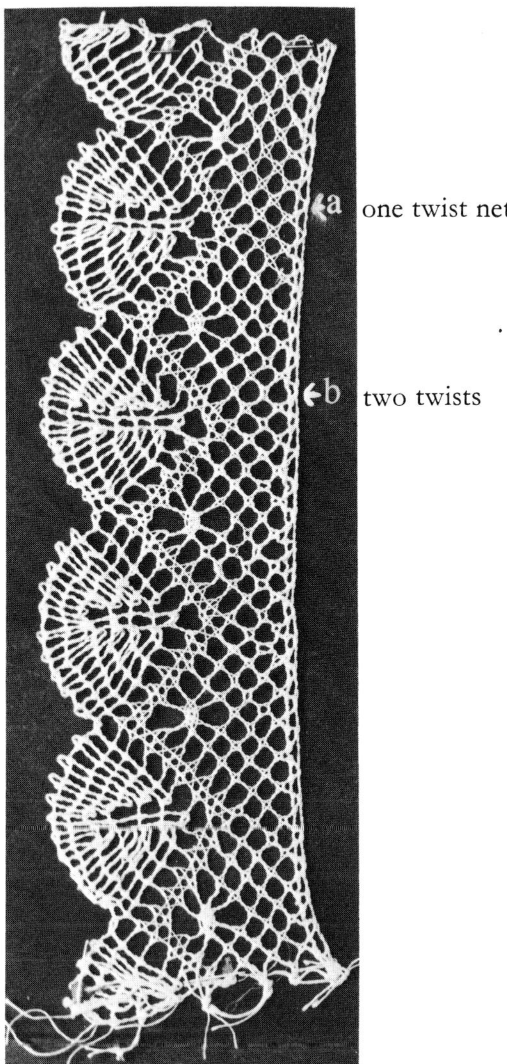

30. Torchon

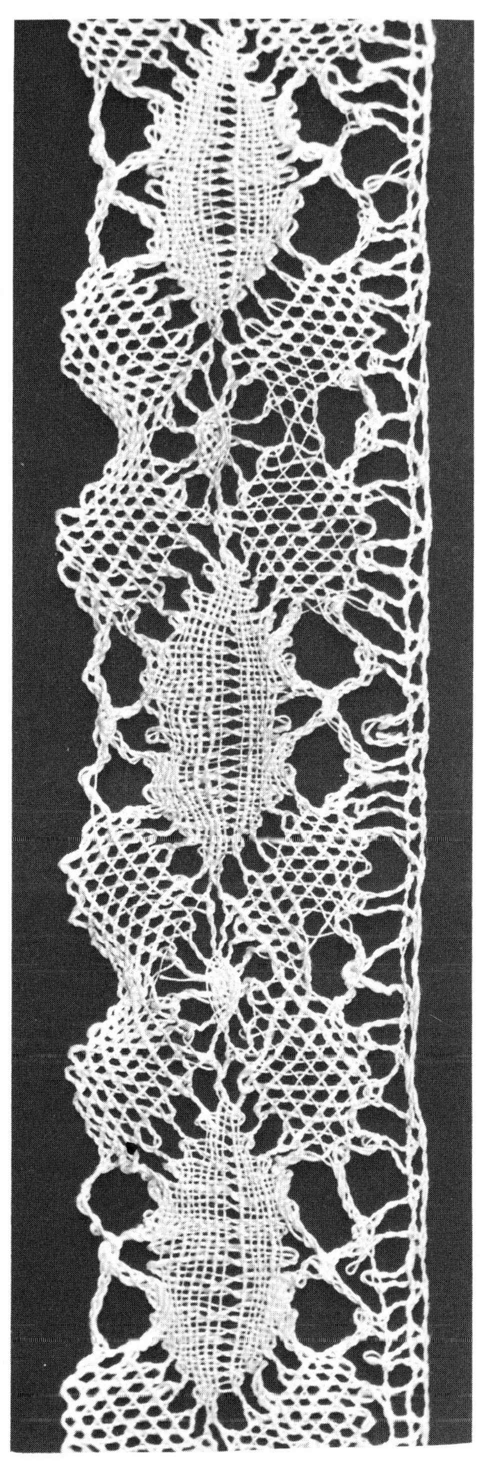

31. Torchon. A beginner's first ever effort.
Note: 1. Uneven twists.
2. Foot loops, etc.
3. The two bars at the head should have had more stitches before the pin hole in the middle where the pairs should have an extra twist round the pin.

It is a good practice to experiment in this way with Torchon, twisting the number of times necessary to cover the distance with a firmly corded bar and leaving no split loops such as are seen on the inner side of the foot in Photo 31, a beginner's piece.

The Foot is worked as follows:

Three prs are hung on at 1, Diagram 35*c*, twist outside pr 3 times, middle and lt pr twice.

Two prs are hung on at 2, twisted twice each side of pin.

Torchon net stitch is worked at 3 with the rt pr from 2 and left from 1.

Rt pr from 3 moves rt, makes wh st with the foot passive pr, tw both twice, wh st with foot pr, tw 2 rt pr, twist lt pr 3 times, pin up under both and close round pin with wh st and 2 twists with lt pr, 3 with rt pr, wh st with passive, tw both twice and leave.

The Fan shape at the head, so typical of Torchon, is worked the same as in the 'Little Fan' in 'Point' with the same variations, or as in sample II (Photo 30), where the direction of the weavers changes to a diagonal line and reverses at the half-way stage, twisting passives and workers as required.

The Trail. This is a diagonal band separating the net from the head or surrounding a block of fancy filling usually done in wh or ½ stitch in various widths. In sample II, 2 pairs are used, 1 weaver, ½ stitch trail.

When turning a corner in a ½ stitch trail it is necessary to gain a pin hole to fill the corner. This is done by working to and enclosing the extreme pin then take up the 2nd pr at the other side of the trail and use it as the new weaver.

In addition to the basic net there are many varieties of fillings that can be used as net ground or as a filling. These usually use the same pricking but some have a few extra holes added. The best of these is Rose Ground in the versions shown on the page of Fillings Nos. 1 to 3. This has an extra hole pricked after drawing in the squares where the 'Rose' is to be.

The Tally (see p. 46.) is used extensively in Torchon in fillings, groups, or lines following or enclosed by trails.

The Spider. A useful stitch providing contrast between weaving and net. It is usually made with 4 prs, but can be made with more, each twisted 3 times to provide long firm legs. The pricking is a square, diamond-wise, with a pin hole in the middle, see Diagrams 38 and 39. Pair 1 is woven wh st through 2 and 3. Pr 4 through 2 and 3, pin up, close round pin, weave rt through rt pr, tw 3 times and take out into net. Weave wh st with 2 lt prs and then 2 middle ones, twist all 3 times and take out to net. It is essential to pull the top legs firm by pulling outwards after putting up the middle pin and the bottom legs when doing the net stitches on the lower edge of the square and not before. The object is to keep the centre, the body of the spider, as wide, flat and shapely as possible.

TORCHON FILLINGS

Rose Ground No. 1

Use 10 to 1 inch graph paper. Prick as for Torchon net. Draw in squares as shown.

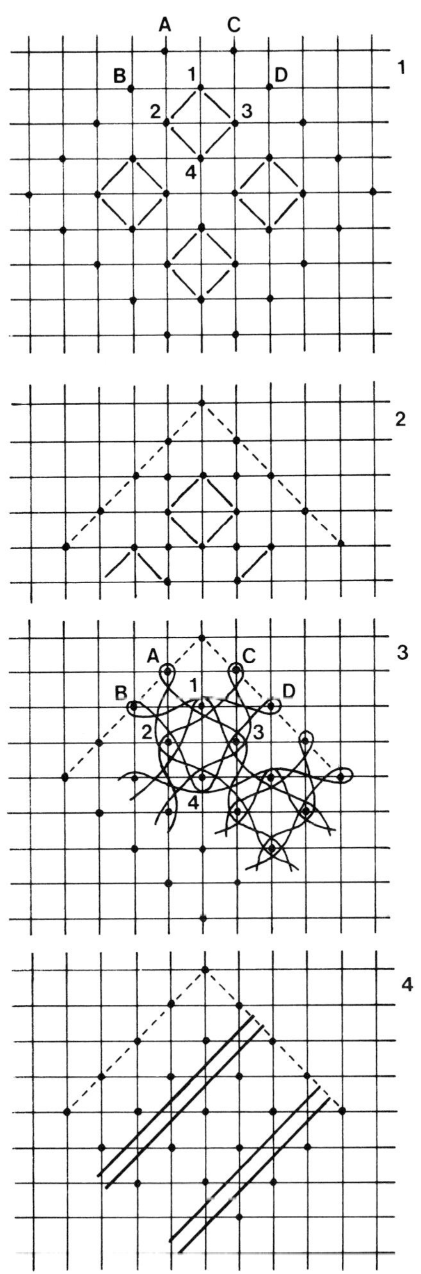

Diagram 40.

Hang on prs and twist at:
A & B and make ½ st
and C & D and make ½ st
Make ½ st at 1 and enclose with ½ st
With 2 lt prs ditto at 2
With 2 rt prs ditto at 3
With 2 middle prs ditto at 4
Make ½ st with 2 lt prs and leave
Make ½ st with 2 rt prs and leave

Rose Ground No. 2

Is made same as No. 1 but an extra hole round the square is pricked where the ½ st is as in No. 1, work a ½ st and close round pin in ½ st.

No. 3

A variant, using the same pricking as No. 2 is made by giving the outside pair all round the Rose 1 extra twist.

No. 4

There are various fillings based on this pricking. The holes are as for No. 1, but 2 parallel lines are drawn between alternate rows. Half or whole stitches straddle the lines, each line can be joined with ½ stitch, twisted bars or rows of Tallies and so a great variety of fillings can be 'collected'.

A variation can be made by doing the twist between each wh st of the body, which gives a lighter effect.

Leaves, grouped as flowers, or little crosses as in Maltese are found in Torchon, and a variant of the Tally worked on top of a ½ or wh st block is often seen. This doubling can be in the form of a leaf lying flat on the weaving or a long tally that is made too long for the space available and is then fastened back into a loop by being woven in. They are made by allowing for 2 extra prs at the top of the area which are woven with the cloth-work prs at the beginning, then moved over for the weaving to be carried on which comes behind the leaf or tally, then bring the extra prs to the middle, work as required, then weave right across with all prs. This is a useful stitch to use in lampshade braids where the extra bit can be done in a different colour. See Chapter 12.

The *Head* edge is made in a variety of ways usually using plaited bars. These can go to the head pin where the lt pr is given an extra twist before pinning up and plaiting back to the lace. Or they can have picots, usually 5 along the outer edge only of the head loop.

Crossing of Bars. Where the pin hole needs to be emphasized an extra twist is given to each pr. When 4 prs are to cross, each pr is put together to be worked as 1 thread, which gives you 4 in all, and the crossing is worked as in normal Torchon ground, so that out of a plait of 4 threads 2 double threads come out, 2 from the other plait, the middle prs are crossed, the side prs twisted, the pin put up, close round it with another cross and twist. Then continue the plait each side as usual.

In flowers and places where 6 or 8 prs have to be crossed the leaves are each finished firmly with a wh st. Then the same principle is used of using the prs as single threads, taking care not to twist the petal. The centres are worked in ½ stitch, then each side. Pin up, work centre prs in ½ stitch and repeat at sides. With 6 leaves the middle at the top works through to the centre bottom. With 8 they work across diagonally to the opposite side.

When joining a plait to a foot, where 2 prs have to join 1 pr, use the workers from the foot, wh st through both pairs from the plait, tw workers, pin up, weave back to continue foot. Where the 4 prs coming in are from a tally or leaf, to prevent this twisting, weave through both prs, pin up between the 2 prs coming from the leaf, leave the worker to continue into the next leaf. Using the lt pr from the leaf close round the pin and continue into the foot, the workers having thus exchanged places.

32. A student's first samples

1. Braid and foot edge in No. 8 Star Sylko
2. Torchon Fan, No. 80 thread
3. Torchon Ribbon insertion
4. Simple edging
5. Spider and Diamond insertion

MALTESE AND CLUNY

These laces are much coarser than those already mentioned, using for pricking 6 or 8 to the inch graph paper and 35 to 50 cotton. Maltese uses the tally pulled tight at each end so that it is pointed, in groups of 4, like a little cross. In 'Bedfordshire Maltese' these crosses are more often square at the ends. The ground is usually the plaited bar with picots. Cluny is characterized by the tallies being elongated into petals and leaves, flowers of 8 or more petals and the leaves arranged fernlike, the ground being plaited bars or Torchon rose ground.

The plaited bars are made with ½ stitch, i.e. cross the middle, tw sides, repeated and pulled firm until the space is filled, keeping the prs spread and the plait untwisted. The picots on these bars can be made with a single thread as in the first part of the proper picot with the bobbin thread under the one coming from the lace, but this *does not keep its twist in use*. The excuse for using the single picot is that the thick thread would be clumsy double. The fact is, that if this is so, too thick a thread is being used. Only the double thread picot, properly made, will keep in place and stand up to washing. The only concession made to the thicker thread is that 3 tw are given before the picot and 1 after. When continuing the plait pull it well up to the picot. The sample shown in Chapter 1 was made by a reasonably competent worker but note the distorted single picots.

The foot can be as in Torchon, especially for the Maltese, but in Cluny sometimes a more elaborate foot can be used such as two passives twisted once between the wh st and the worker twisted 3 times between the two passives, which has the effect of pushing them further apart and tightening the foot pin hole and, more important, the snatch pin hole often seen in the long spaces that come between the ground prs. These pin holes on the inner side of the foot that are not worked into the ground at a catch pin as in 'Point' need to be twisted adequately – at least 3 times – before putting up the pin. The loop should not show separate threads.

For other examples of these laces see Chapter 1, page 14.

33. Black 'Cluny' type lace, probably made in Bucks

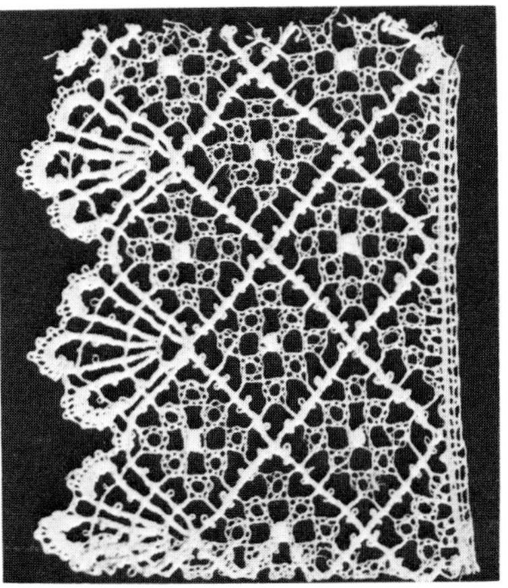

34. Torchon. Rose ground with tallies

9. Corners

Often one comes across straight patterns of lace edgings but rarely one with a corner, but a corner is always useful to have whether for a 'point' handkerchief or Torchon table mat.

A Point Lace corner is not easy to design as the angle of the ground is 52° so there is always a space to be filled somehow on the turn. In other words, to design round the corner not merely the filling of the angle is necessary, but the enlarging of the outer area at *b* (Diagram 41). The corner must be worked (to look right) across the corner (*b* and *d*), i.e. the pillow has to be turned at an angle. In the diagram the direction of the weaving is indicated. It is sometimes possible to keep the crossway working to the sections *b* and *d* but it often looks better to include *a* and *c* as well. The best method of doing this is to bring a part of the pattern surrounded by gimp (*d*) down to the foot pins, plot the net holes up to this, then turn the pattern to plot the corner on the diagonal, pivoting the design on the foot pin. It is not necessary to have a full 'bud' shape on the inner corner. Sometimes the gimp line is brought down to the pin hole above the corner catch pin, a row of honeycomb holes are then pricked in a line with this and the gimp line taken back to the corner bud.

It will be found that extra prs will be needed to cover the extra area round the outside. Don't starve the lace by trying to 'make do' with the prs you have got. Make 'False Purls' at the top purl pins as needed by hanging on two pairs 5 times twisted on the pin and closing round it with a wh st. Use the inner pr into the lace. Take the lt pr to the next purl. At places where there are too many prs carry them along with the gimps and finally take them out within the weaving outside the gimp at the bottom of the final curve(s) of the corner. It may be necessary to hang on and take out another pr of gimps. It is better to plan the pattern so as to avoid this.

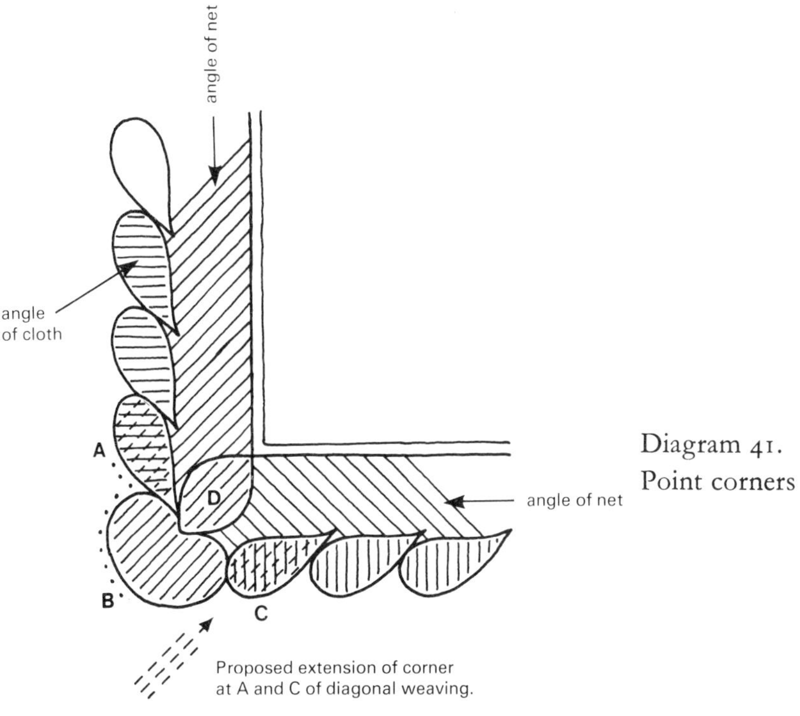

Diagram 41.
Point corners

35. Two alternative corners for Duke's Garter, and corner for Butterfly.

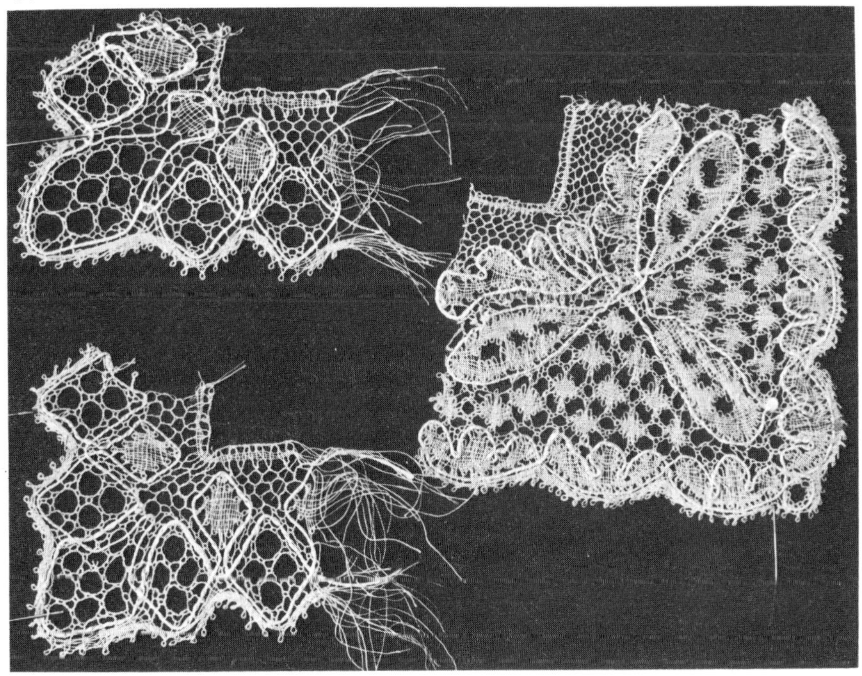

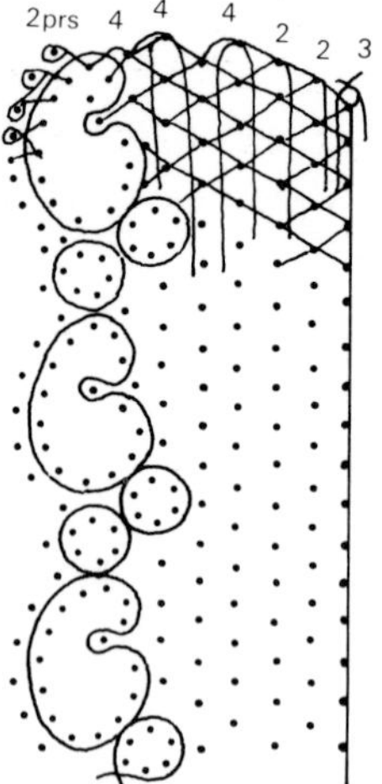

HALF-STITCH 'BEAN' with Kat stitch ground — often worked in black. Bean can be worked in wh. st.

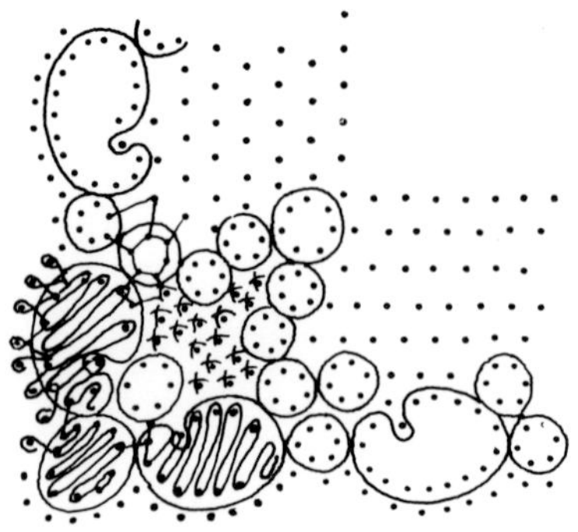

CORNER TURN
Hang extra prs as necessary and gain on a pin

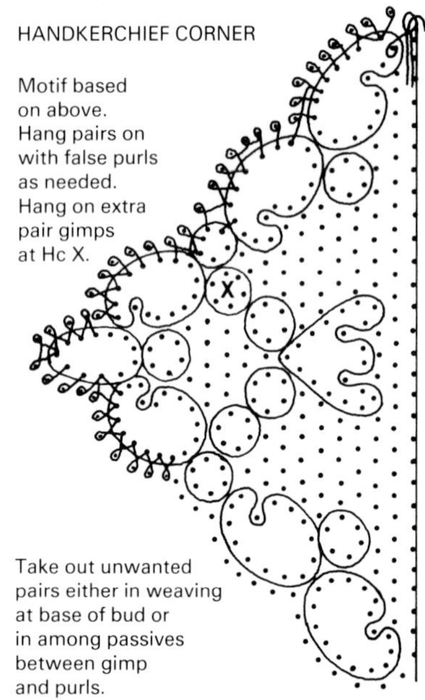

HANDKERCHIEF CORNER

Motif based on above. Hang pairs on with false purls as needed. Hang on extra pair gimps at Hc X.

Take out unwanted pairs either in weaving at base of bud or in among passives between gimp and purls.

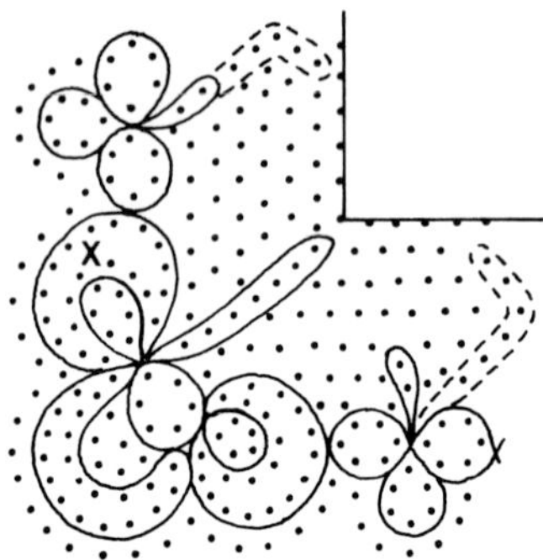

CORNER FOR TRUE LOVER'S KNOT.
The dotted lines show the suggested gimpline for conversion to corner only.
Hang pn extra gimp pair at x

Diagram 42.

Torchon corners are quite simple to plan as the net is angled at 45°. A small bag mirror helps to find the right place to do this in a running pattern. It will be found that a reversal of the direction of a diagonal trail is often needed at the corner and again possibly in the middle of a side in order to bring the lace to the next corner at a convenient slope.

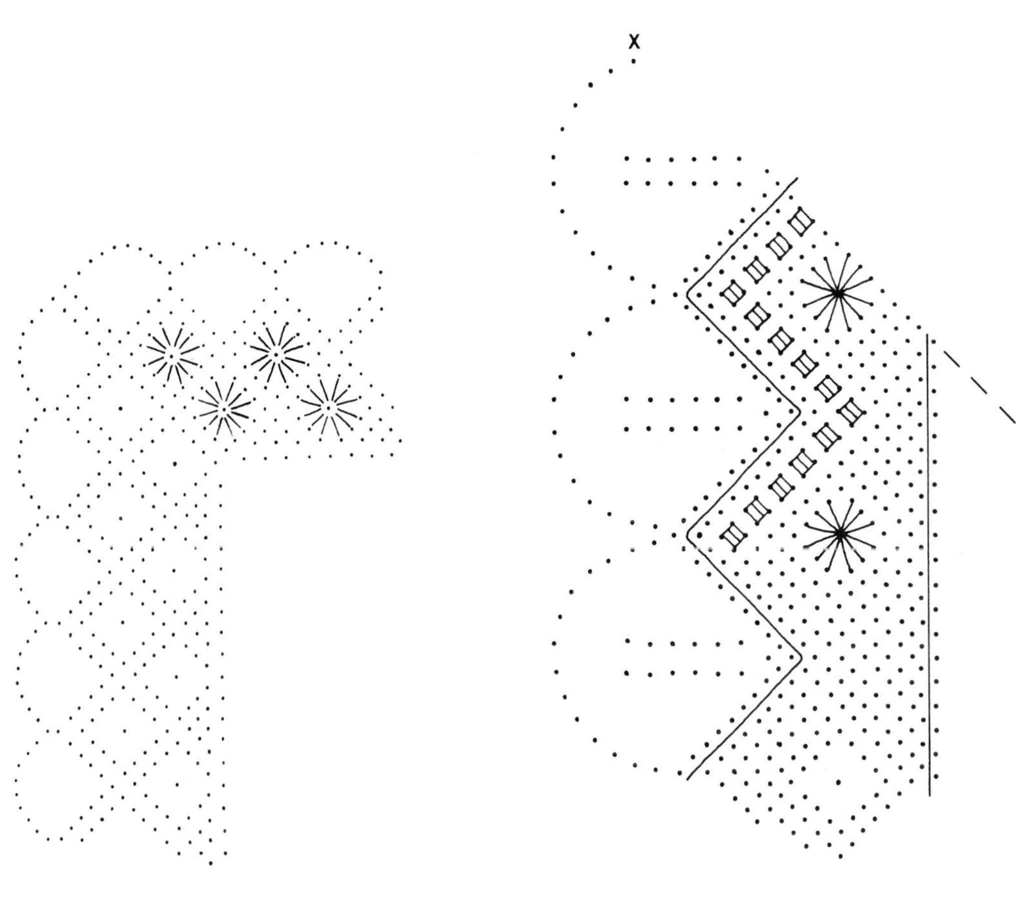

Diagram 43. Torchon Corner. The pattern may be pricked, cut across the corner at 45° and reversed, adjusting the outer curve at X.

36. Corner. Old Water Lily Pattern, Bucks Point

10. *Danish 'Tönder' and Swedish Lace*

This fine lace is basically 'Point' or Lille together with some *Torchon* techniques. The Tönder is made with a very fine thread (250) but a thicker gimp than is usual with point. Four and six pin Hc rings occur frequently and the gimp is used not only to outline shapes but also in many little fernlike shapes as in 'Frostings' and fillings.

The ground can be *Torchon* ½ stitch with one or two twists between the pin holes or Point ground – for the finer threads. The motifs can be filled by ½ or wh st weaving, as in point, and Torchon tallies and spiders are used even with the point ground. Honeycomb is also used but is referred to in these laces as 'rose ground'. There is a regularity in their patterns that is very reminiscent of Swedish embroidery, the clusters of Hc rings usually being in twos or fours, the heads often being as straight as the foot except for the purl pins. Existing patterns for this lace are all for the fine thread, so graph paper will have to be used to enlarge the pricking to suit the thread available as for the point patterns. In the pricking of Rikke, the handkerchief corner, 150–120 thread can be used with a sufficiently strongly contrasted gimp. 10 to 1 inch graph paper was used.

Very many of the gimps lie parallel with each other and therefore must be carefully worked with a controlling twist between them such as between the Hc head and the four pin rings in Ex. 1 and in 'Laberinth'. Another characteristic is the very frequent use of nook pins as in Example No. 2 'Heart and Spider' which also uses the Torchon spider with 6 legs. Watch the gimp carefully in this pattern. The outside gimp of the spider goes closely round the heart and the inside stays on that side all the time. It will be found easier to draw in the former first throughout and then the latter. When working, the gimps are crossed on completing the spider, then the heart is worked and the gimps cross before beginning on the next spider.

The 2 pin holes in the V of the head side are both worked in Hc.

In the insertion called 'Frosting' there are no problems. The pin hole at the top and bottom of the wh st bud is worked as a Hc st. The 2 pin holes at the centre of the Hc bud are worked as Hc chain, i.e. 3 Hc sts with no pin in the middle one.

In Swedish Torchon all the usual Torchon stitches are used but this lace is characterized by the use of gimp which surrounds whole or ½ stitch lozenges and 4-pin honeycomb rings. See the Bibliography for available Swedish books.

37. 'Rikke'

HEART AND SPIDER*

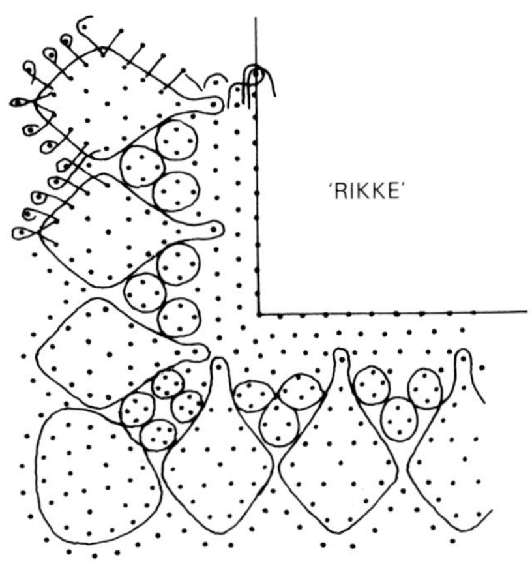

17 prs plus extra for corner
1 pr gimp

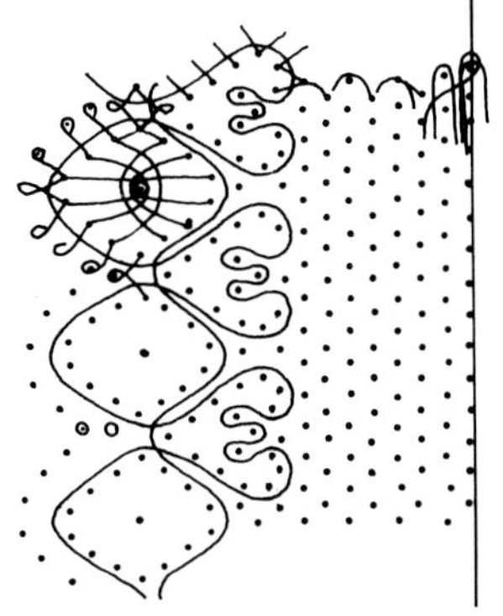

22prs. 1 pr gimp

LABYRINTH*
as designed for 250 thread

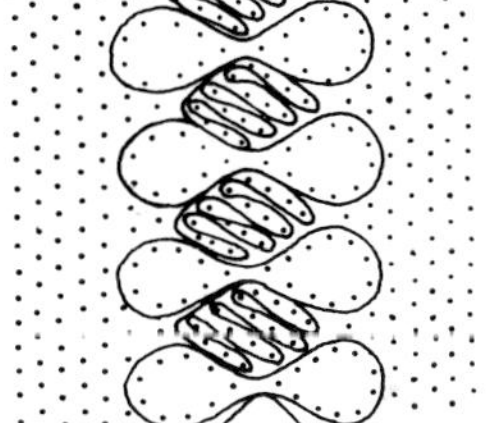

as enlarged for 100 thread

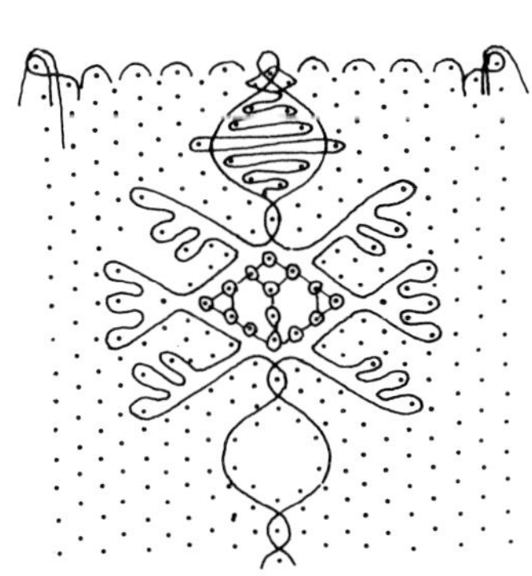

INSERTION: 'FROSTINGS'*

26 prs. 1 pr gimp
N.B. Weaving in the wh. st. bud is taken through gimp in middle.

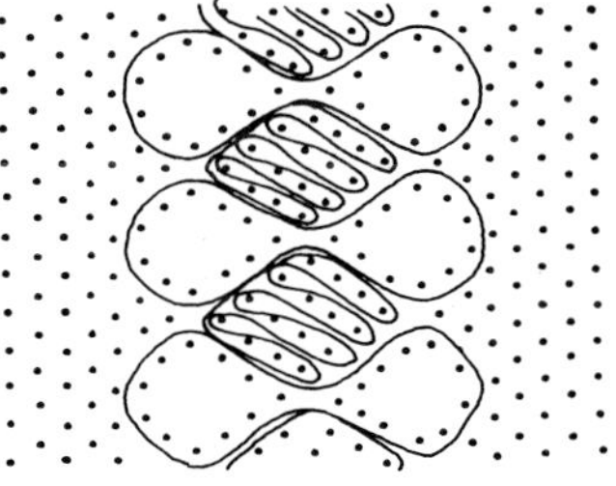

*From *Knipling Efter Tegning* by Johanne Byrop-Larson

Diagram 44. Tönder laces

38. Honiton. Photographed from the wrong side but as worked to show rolled threads carried across from one shape to the next. Note Tally leaves pointed in this piece, as in many others of the same date. (See note to diagrams, page 87.)

11. Honiton and Brussels

In Honiton and Brussels laces most of the stitches described in the preceding chapters are used but there are fundamental differences in their use and application. Detailed instructions for making these laces are beyond the scope of this book as there are many variations of holes and of veinings in the cloth work and in the fillings. The fundamental stitches follow and a few descriptive drawings and photos. A thorough knowledge of the previous chapters and the use of a magnifying glass on any good examples would provide all the information necessary for any but the grandest lace.

The thread must be very fine, at least 140.

The pillow is round, board based, but at least 4″ high and about 12″–14″ wide to enable the bobbins to be moved around as the pattern is worked in all directions. See Diagram 45(1).

The bobbins are pointed at their bottom end (see Diagram 45(2*a*)) to enable 'sewings' to be made, i.e. they are joined on to parts of the lace in prs by pulling the loop of the thread between prs through the foot pin hole and passing the other bobbin through this loop end first.

The '*needle pin*' with which the loop is pulled through is our old friend the 'pricker' with the shoulder of the dowelling whittled down to make it easier to get closer to the hole. See Diagram 45(2*b*).

The parts of the pattern that form the outer edges of the article has purl pins worked as in 'Point' but the Devon workers usually do 7 twists instead of 5. The other edges are made as in a 'Point' foot which gives the necessary holes for sewings, the pin being put up *before* the wh st is made.

The design, or as much of it as can conveniently be worked on the pillow, is drawn on pricking card. This can be almost any little floret, sprig, leaf, ribbon

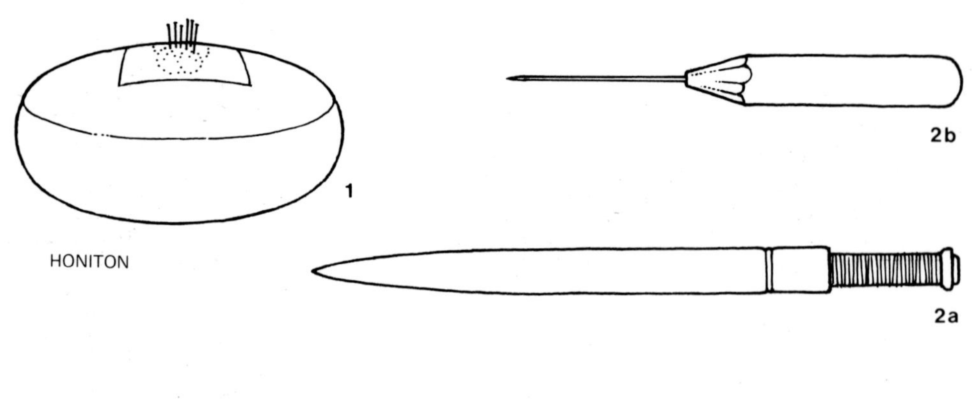

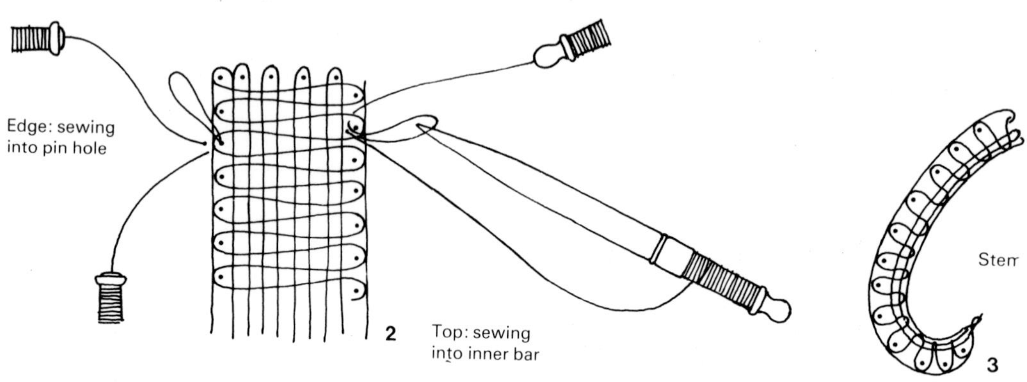

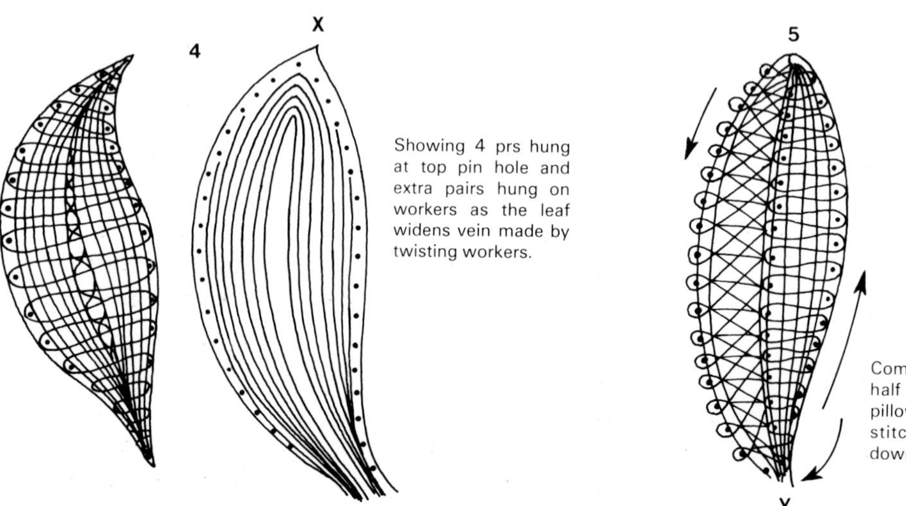

Diagram 45. Honiton

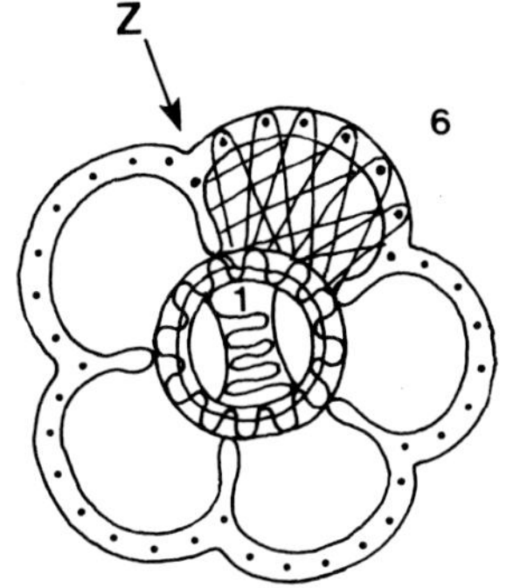

Stem ring. Half-stitch petal 'Foot' outer edge. Cotton or gimp used as last thread just inside footholes. Tally in middle. The *inner* pinholes or petals are not holes but sewings into edge of stem.

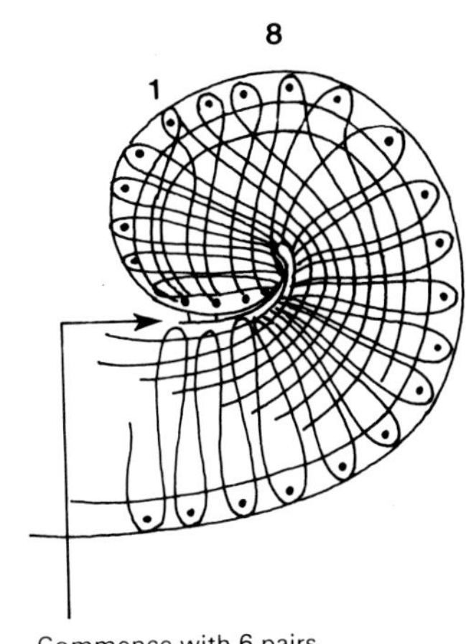

Commence with 6 pairs

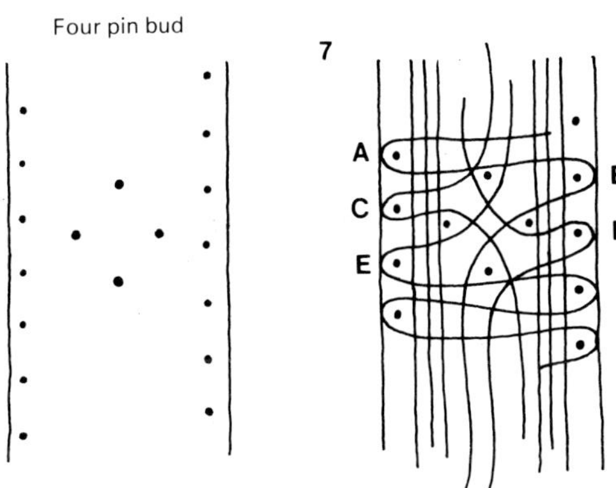

Diagram 45. Honiton

bow, etc., in any convenient shape taking into consideration only the flow of the *internal* cloth work, i.e. wh st threads and gimps. The pin holes are pricked along the outline at about one-twentieth inch intervals. *No* thought has to be given to inflow and outward movements from the net as in Point as the net and other filling bobbins are sewn on as described above and as required, worked directionally as in the other laces and taken out with a sewing and tied off, when they have reached the end of their work on the other side of the space to be filled.

The pattern of sprigs is completed first. To enable the work to follow the curves, etc. the pins of the completed parts are pushed right down to the lace and a piece of transparent parchment or plastic, about 4″ × 2″, used under the bobbins but over any work completed. See Photo 42 in Appendix A.

When ready to do the net and/or fillings the pins are raised and withdrawn when a sewing is made but replaced immediately afterwards to prevent any distortion during working. Sewings must be made through the pin holes and not through the intermediate bars of the foot for edge sewing but into the side bars when top sewing over a stem.

This lace has a right and wrong side and is made face down so that the tying out can be done not to show and therefore the passives from one part can sometimes be rolled together and carried over to the next place of use.

A thick thread is used round the edge of cloth work but is worked in with it and not separated by twists as in Point. To enable the cloth work to be done evenly a thread pr is hung on with the thick pr thus forming an extra pr each side of the leaf.

This thicker thread, often called 'the cotton', is sometimes 2 or 3 of the lace threads used as one, i.e. strands wound together on to the bobbin, but looks better if an ordinary No. 50 2 cord cotton is used.

One of the most important stitches to learn that has not been done before is the *stem* or '*Ten stick*'. This lace is sometimes called 'Ten stick lace'. It is used for outlines, 'raised work' such as in leaf veins, to make stems, tendrils, little outlined flowers, buds, rings, etc. Five pairs (hence ten stick) are used, a foot pair, 1 pair weavers and 3 passives. It has foot holes down one side only, on the outer edge of the curve, the weaver going to the other edge, making a turning stitch and returning to the foot without any pin holes being made. By pulling the inner pr, which has been left behind quite tight, a corner can be turned or by leaving it loose a straight line made. The very slight gap made by the twist at the edge is useful, especially if it has an extra twist, for sewing in pairs. Some workers use 2 wh st for this turn, and then a wh st plus a ½ stitch, leave outside pr using other pr as worker.

The scroll, Diagram 45(8), is another characteristic shape. Hang on the required number of prs where indicated. When the centre knob has been worked, about at 1 work back 3 prs and leave the workers to lie and use the other pr of this last stitch as workers to proceed to the edge where the edge stitch is worked and leaders dropped. Bring the next unworked passive pr through to the edge, work stitch and drop and so on until the unworked passives have been worked to the edge. Continue as for braid, making some turns on a pin to keep the workers working straight across the braid.

Leaves or large petals are sometimes worked as at Diag. 45(4), by hanging on 6 or 8 prs at the top point X, weaving to rt pr and adding on any extra required at the outer edge as the leaf proceeds.

Or as at Diag. 45(5) where the work begins at Y by hanging on about 3 prs making a foot edge down the centre and turning (see Turns, page 44.) at the top. Turn the pillow and work back to the bottom in ½ stitch making sewings through the edge pin holes in the centre vein.

The *flower* at Diag. 45 (6) is commenced by making a ring of Ten stick, tie off but do not cut. Carry these 5 prs, hanging on 2 or 3 others at any point such as Z. Sew on a cotton and a bobbin at the centre at 1, work through all prs to outer edge, take up innermost pr and work ½ stitch through to foot pin at Z working the cotton as the last bobbin in the weaving. Work the petal until full, weave the cotton through to centre, sew on to centre ring and weave out again to next edge hole. When the last petal has been worked, sew off or roll enough pairs for a Ten stick stem, easing to edge at Z, and do the stem.

Diag. 45 (7), *Four-pin bud*. This is a fancy hole found in braids and leaves. It is marked on the pricking with 4 pin holes in the middle of the petal, braid or leaf.

The leader A is taken through to B and back to 1 pr short of the middle and tw 3. The next pr tw 3. The next pr weaves out to C and back to 1 pr short of the middle, tw 3, also twist remaining middle pr 3 times, thus having 4 tw prs hanging in the middle space.

Put pin in middle hole and close with wh st round pin, tw 3 with both middle prs. Work wh st plus 3 tw with lt-hd prs and rt-hd prs, put up pins in side holes outside both wh sts. Make wh st, plus 3 tw with 2 middle prs and put pin between them. With rt twisted pr of the middle 2 work out to edge hole D, back through the rt middle pr and leave hanging down as a passive. With left twisted pr weave left to edge hole E and back through all other prs to opposite edge hole and continue the weaving as before taking care to settle the passives at the side of the little hole snugly round it to avoid spaces in the bottom corners. This little hole is peculiar to Honiton lace and very rarely, if ever, found in Brussels.

SEWING OFF

At the end of a leaf or motif, having taken out a few prs as the shape decreases, sew the edge pr.into the last hole on the edge to which it is to join, tie off 3 times. With runners weave through remaining prs to other side, work wh st with outside pr, sew and tie off 3 times. Take out any 'cotton' prs. Do not knot. Tie together all other prs in prs, place *all* inside the tied runners, wrap these round the bunch and tie off 3 times. Cut all off close leaving any needed to be used in a nearby area in a roll wrapped round by the runners which will then be used to sew in the top of the roll in its starting point, but only do this if it can be carried *over* the lace already made and therefore coming on the wrong side. Which brings us to *Raised Work*, i.e. the use of these rolls and the Ten stick as veining and raised edges, etc. It is a complicated and difficult part of this lace and needs to be demonstrated in class. The Ten stick is done first, the roll taken back up it, sewn in, the bobbins then turned back down the leaf and woven as in the free leaf but on the stem edge it is '*Top sewn*' to the foot edge of the Ten stick. Good eyes and a very steady hand are needed. Tuition under expert teachers is arranged by the Devon Education Authority based on Exeter.

The scrolls, braids, sprigs, etc. having been assembled as a pattern on a card the ground is then worked in. The angle of the ground must be kept uniform throughout the piece. If 'point' net is used prick it in. If plaited bars with picots are used draw the lines of the plaits in and keep them as much as possible to a pattern of diagonal lines with all picots on one side only. The sprigs can be appliquéd on to machine-made net but this is not a desirable practice except for large areas such as a wedding veil. It is inexcusable used on small pieces.

Some fillings are given here – there are many more. Their regular appearance depends very largely on choosing the right spot into which to sew the prs needed to fill what is often an irregularly shaped space. There will be much sewing on of prs and taking them out with a sewing and 2 ties, so make sure when sewing on that there is enough thread free of knots to reach the sewing off place as knots spoil any net work.

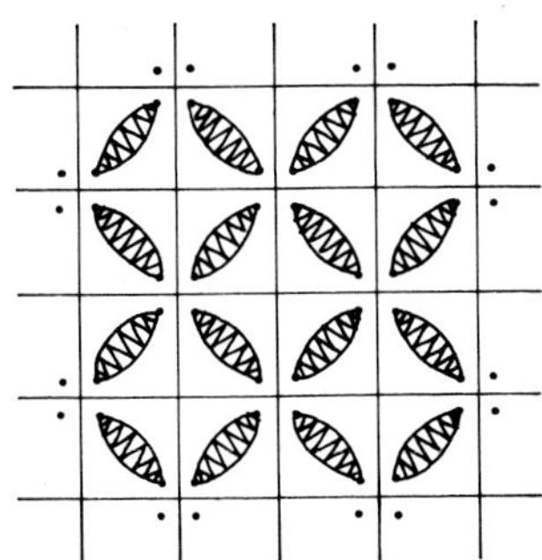

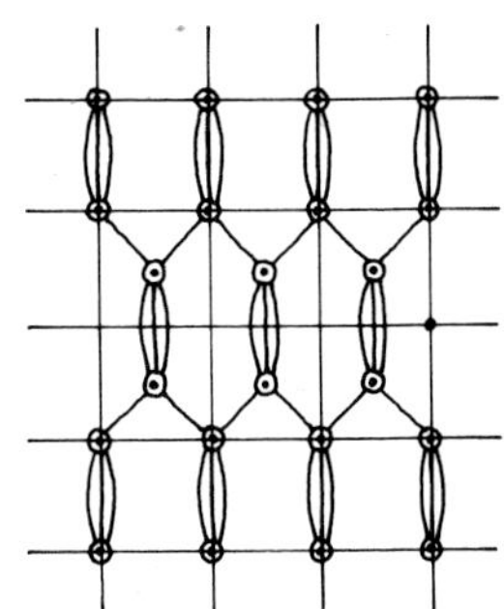

Diamond Filling
Put up pin at end of each tally. Make wh st with middle prs, outer prs and bottom prs, outer prs and bottom prs, putting pin up for tops of next tallies between R and L prs.
Three twists are made with each pair after tallies and whole stitches.
The size in the pricking will be in $\frac{1}{12}$″, i.e. the sides each of these squares = $\frac{1}{12}$″.

Pin Filling
Each pin hole is enclosed by a wh st and 3 tw with 3 tw joining the intervening rows. Looks well worked on $\frac{1}{16}$″ graph paper.
Work each row straight across before commencing next row.

The above two fillings are diagrammed as in the Old Honiton No. 38 and as taught to me by an old Honiton worker. The Tallies are now made square-ended which does give a different effect. The same square-ended 'leads' in Tallies appear in many of the old Bedfordshire mixed laces in the Luton museum.

Purl filling

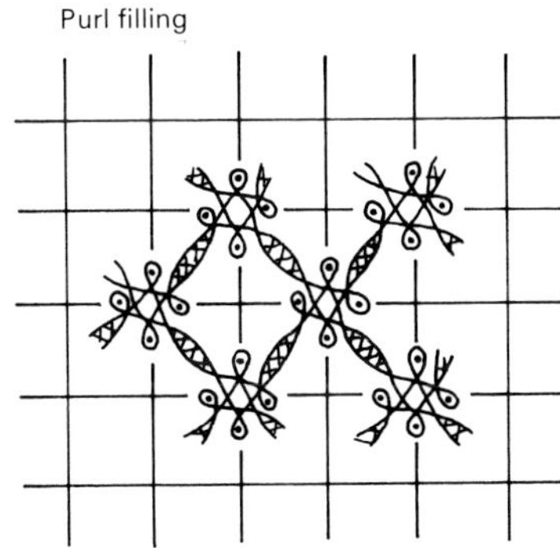

4 prs

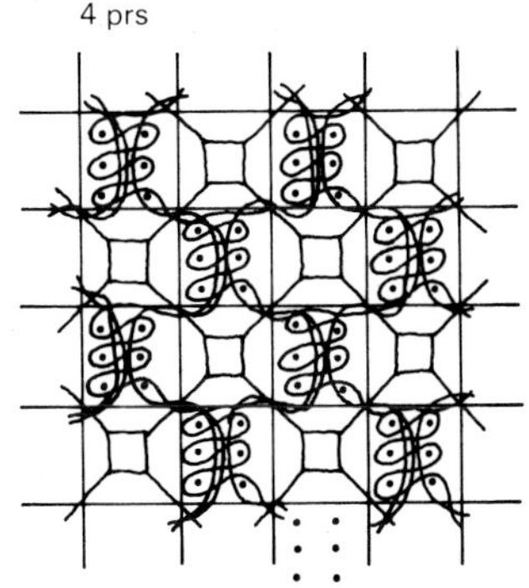

Purl Filling
Half stitch bars. Purl pins round a wh st centre as in 'diamond'.
Note difference in pricking.

Toad in the Hole
Blocks of six pin weaving done with four pairs interspersed with tallies with two pairs each.
Work horizontally using Rt pr each time as weavers for each block. Make wh st bars between blocks passing tally pairs through bars in wh st.

Diagram 46. Honiton Fillings

Diagram 47. Uses of lace

12. General Notes on Present Use, Mounting, Finishing

Present fashions in furniture and dress are showing trends towards lace, braids and fringes, such as we have not seen for decades, and most of these can be made with pillow and bobbin. Frilled shirt fronts and cuffs are very suited to point or fine torchon and the Cluny and Maltese in bright colours and lurex threads for adorning Kaftans and evening clothes can be exciting to play with.

Those who make their own lampshades can also make the braids and fringes they require in the colour they want – ornamental, with metal or lurex, or plain and severe, the most difficult to find in any special colour.

Lace in varying colours and threads can be used in modern embroidery to provide a contrast to coarse modern materials, such as linen and felts.

In lace today we are venturing into the use of threads that the traditionalists would deplore. As long as one does not try to make the new threads do things for which they are not suited but do the things they can. Nylon is too stretchy and slippery to hold in place. Terylene does hold in place and is pleasant to work with but it is very difficult to get the hitch to hold on the bobbin and it cannot hold a purl pin. So in using this thread the snatch pin head, as shown in 'Little Fan', is employed. This would also hold good for most of the man-made threads. See Diagram 50 and Photo 40.

Lace for fashion, just as for more lasting needs, should always be lightly but firmly attached so that it may be unpicked and used again should the fashion change or the lawn of the collar or handkerchief wear out. The author has in her possession a point ground handkerchief from which remains of at least three centres were taken when it was remounted. The article is 150 years old but not a thread of the lace is broken. Many noble laces can be seen in family portraits and, later, in press photographs, being used and re-used in different ways.

The attachment of the lace to an article is very important. Fine lace edgings are easily damaged in two ways – by breaking loose and then tearing (because of insecure sewing) or by being cut when unpicking because of too firm attaching.

METHODS

1: Whip on to a rolled or folded edge, such as the outer edge of a hem. A delightful article can be made, collar or handkerchief, by designing an Italian Hem that mirrors the main shape of the lace and whipping the lace to the outer fold.

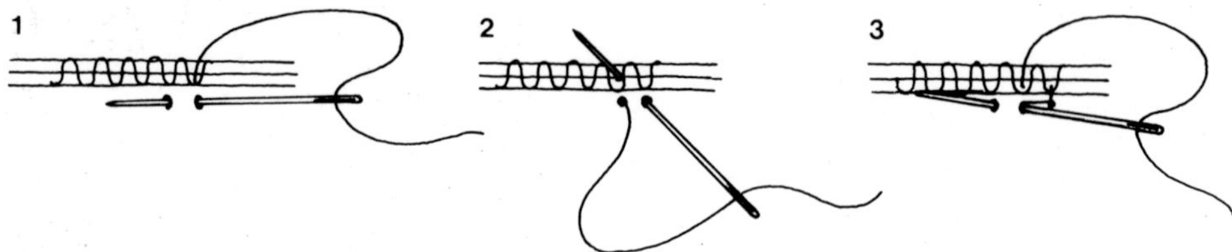

Diagram 48. Pin Stitch

2: *Pin stitch.* This takes a firm hold of the linen or lawn but has only 1 stitch into the lace at the foot pin hole and therefore is easy to cut loose. It consists of 2 stitches into the same holes of the cloth parallel to the lace edge and 1 stitch into the pin hole coming out at the forward pin stitch hole in the cloth. Triangular stitch endangers the foot passives. The lace should be tacked on the straight of the thread about the depth of the foot into the cloth. After the pin stitching is done cut cloth closely away at the back. If the weave is loose leave 2 or 3 threads in depth and very lightly, using lace thread, whip these back into the pin stitches taking care not to obscure the holes of either the lace or the pin stitches.

If the edge of the article is finished by any of the forms of square stitch it is better to whip on to the *outer* edge as a separate operation.

N.B.

It quite spoils the effect of the lace to stitch the foot inside the cloth, leaving the foot braid obscured. It gives the lace an incomplete appearance and is very clumsy to look at. All of the lace must be seen if it is to be seen at all. Braids, on the other hand, can, of course, be applied on top of cloth. Therefore the rule would be – if seen through all must be seen through – if applied keep all within the cloth work.

39. The Attachment of Lace

MOUNTING

It is very important when mounting lace to match the lace with the cloth to get a correct balance. Point laces using fine thread should only be stitched to the finest linen, Terylene lawn or most delicate cambric. Torchon can be mounted on table linens but not too heavy a variety. Cluny and Maltese, in which a heavier thread is often used, can be attached to really heavy linen.

When appliquéing Honiton sprigs to a wedding veil try to match the net to the lace. A round-holed net looks better than a diamond weave but if it is a choice of weight, choose the finest even if the net is not ideal. If the net is too coarse the delicacy of the lace stitches is lost and the holes and other spaces are confused. Use the lace thread itself to do the appliqué stitches.

When using lace across the end of an article such as on a hand-towel or the end of a necktie, the ends of the lace need careful planning. Do not hem the *lace* and leave it so. Two methods are suggested in the sketches below. The aim is to attach the raw edges of the lace firmly to the cloth, having finished it off as in method *b*, Chapter 4, when it can be pin stitched to cloth or enclosed in a narrow hem or binding. The application of the edging would involve setting the lace to its own depth into the cloth and cutting away after stitching.

Always when using lace try to keep it in as long a piece as possible remembering it may be used again, perhaps in different ways, by your granddaughter!

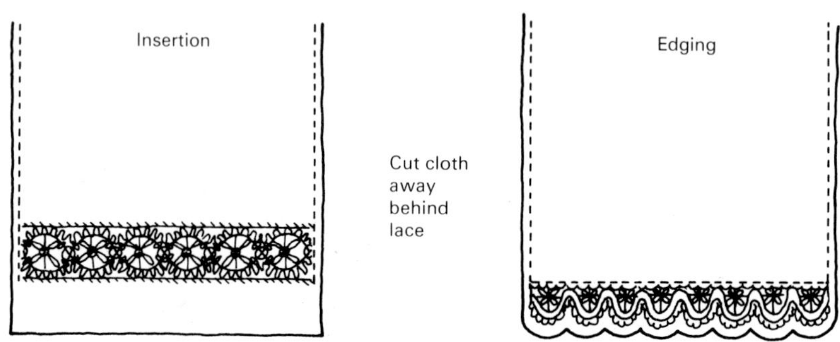

Diagram 49. Using lace across the ends of an article

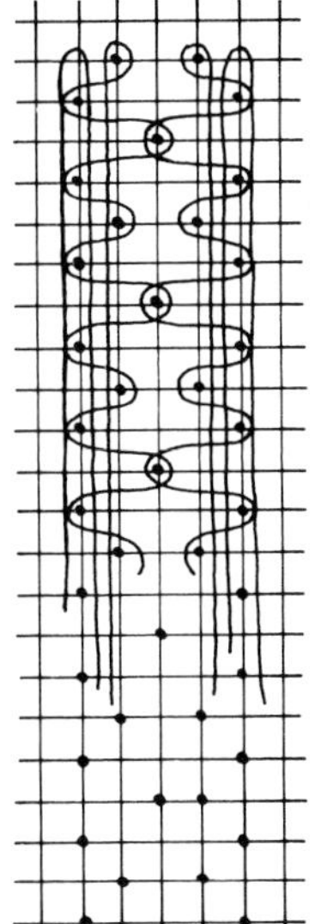

Diagram 50*a*. Insertion. 4 prs, can be threaded with baby ribbon or lurex.

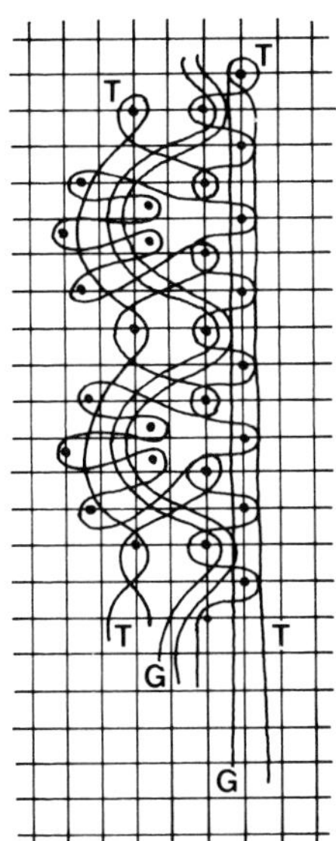

Diagram 50*b*. Braid for lampshades 4 prs thread, T. 1 pr + 1 single, gold silk, G.

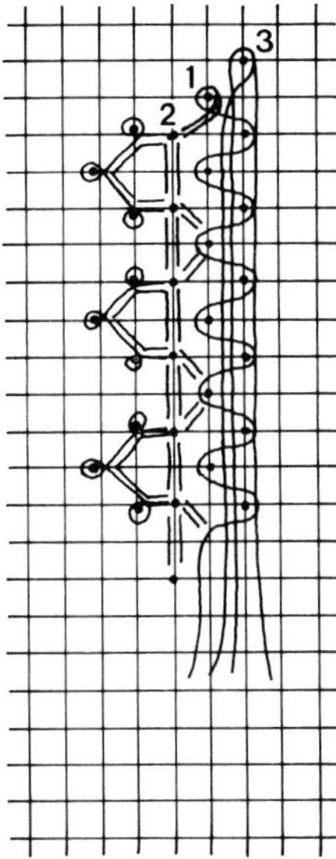

Diagram 50*c*. 'Ninepin' edging 8 prs bobbins = $\frac{1}{2}$ st plait. Hang 3 prs on 1. 2 prs on 2. 3 prs on 3.

40. Students' Braid and Fringe

Appendix A: Pillows

For first lessons the board types are adequate. Using any board – preferably 'hard board' – take a piece approximately 14″ × 18″. Make a bag of closely woven linen or cotton cloth, dark green or blue about ½″ bigger all round. Seam 3 sides, slip in board and stuff very hard on one side of the board only with wheat straw, well hammered till smooth and firm, and stitch up with strong thread. This is only suitable for learning stitches, braid, etc. as the lace has to be unpinned and moved up when the bottom of the pillow is reached.

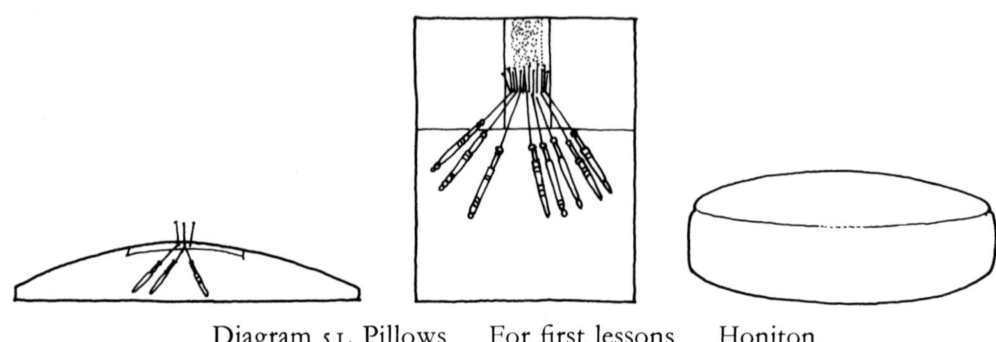

Diagram 51. Pillows For first lessons Honiton

THE DEVON PILLOW

The pillow consists of 2 rounds of material joined by a strip 3″ to 4″ wide and stuffed hard with straw. In photograph 42 the piece of plastic (see p. 83) has been moved over to show how the sprigs are made separately. Note how the threads on the left have caught on a pin.

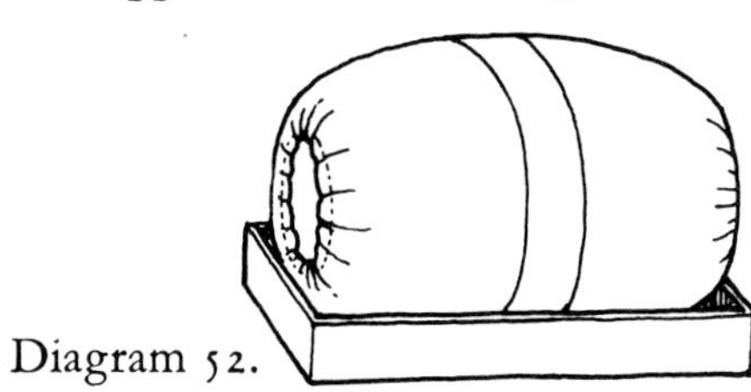

Diagram 52.

BOLSTER PILLOW

This is the most usual type used by old Buckinghamshire and Bedfordshire workers. A piece of material, stout and closely woven, 20″ × 30″ is required. Seam the short sides together. Hem ($\frac{3}{4}$″) the long. With strong tape gather up and tie one end leaving a hole about 5″ in diameter. Cut 2 circles of material and 2 circles of strong card about 8″ in diameter. Place one of each, cloth first, in the bottom of the bag thus formed and stuff and stuff, hammer and stuff until *tight*, using wheat or barley straw. Chaff shifts about and sawdust soon packs down. Place card and cloth on top, gather in and tie off tight to match the other end. Use a seed box, cleaned and covered with cloth as a stand and receptacle for spare cotton, scissors, etc.

It will be found that after about a week a further half sack of straw can be packed into the pillow! Roll well to get smooth.

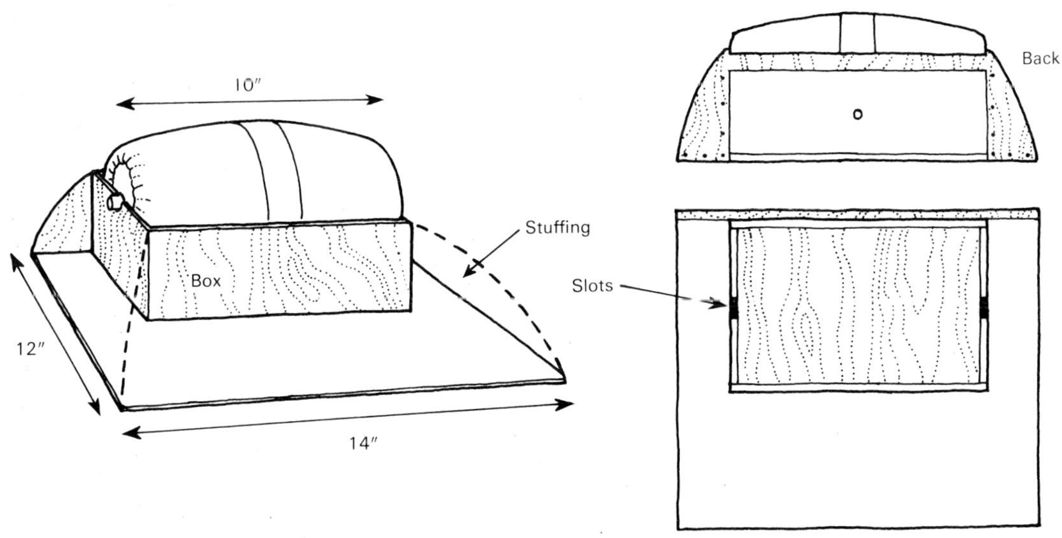

Diagram 53. French pillow

'FRENCH' PILLOW

This consists of a small bolster about 10″ long and 10″ in circumference on a wooden spindle which rests in slots on the side of a box with cushioned sides and a board base. The straw in the bolster is usually packed longitudinally and the final tightening done by driving the spindle (½″ dowelling) through the middle. This spindle should be about ¾″ longer each end than the little bolster. The box with slots cut to take the spindle is nailed to the back of a board base sufficiently wide to take a good spread of bobbins when the space between the box and board is stuffed – a good size would be about 14″ × 12″. At the back a piece of wood with a piece cut out to take a drawer for bobbins, etc. is nailed right across having first removed the bottom half of the back of the box. Do not remove the whole of the back of the box as the space between the 2 pieces of wood, i.e. box and back plank, forms a useful anchorage for pins holding a pocket for the lace which is finished. The drawer which must be shallow enough to be clear of the bottom of the bolster, is often made of a cigar or candy box with a piece of wood or card, bigger than the opening, fixed on the front with a centre knob for pulling out. A piece of stout material large enough to cover all and turn under 2″ all round is then placed on top. The box part to hold the bolster, is cut out allowing ¾″ turnings and the material securely and closely tacked with *brass* tacks well driven home all round the top edge of the box. The sides and back are then fairly loosely tacked down underneath the board and the stuffing begins from the front. Almost anything can be used for this as long as it is flat and firm at the finish and will take stored pins as a pincushion. It does not have to take the firm upstanding pins that is the case with the bolster. When thoroughly stuffed all over tack down the front and all round the sides and back, taking in any surplus pleating at the back and tucking in some stuffing round the back plank where it is often useful to stick spare pins or for pinning down the dust cover. Finally neatly cover the bottom making sure no tacks are standing proud of the material when they might scratch a table top. A strip of tough tape, ribbon or fold of material is then attached at the corners and each side of the spindle only on the top edge of the box to cover all tacks and keep the bolster in place by covering the slotted space.

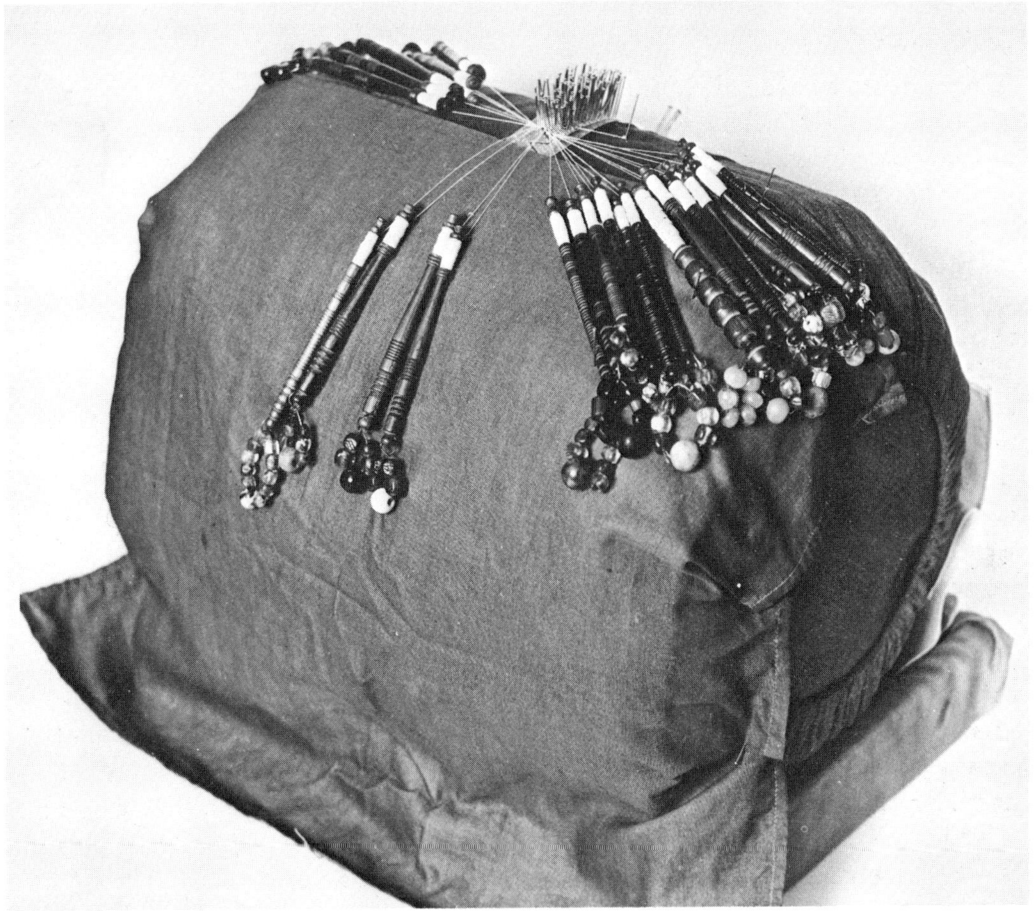

41. Bolster pillow ready for work

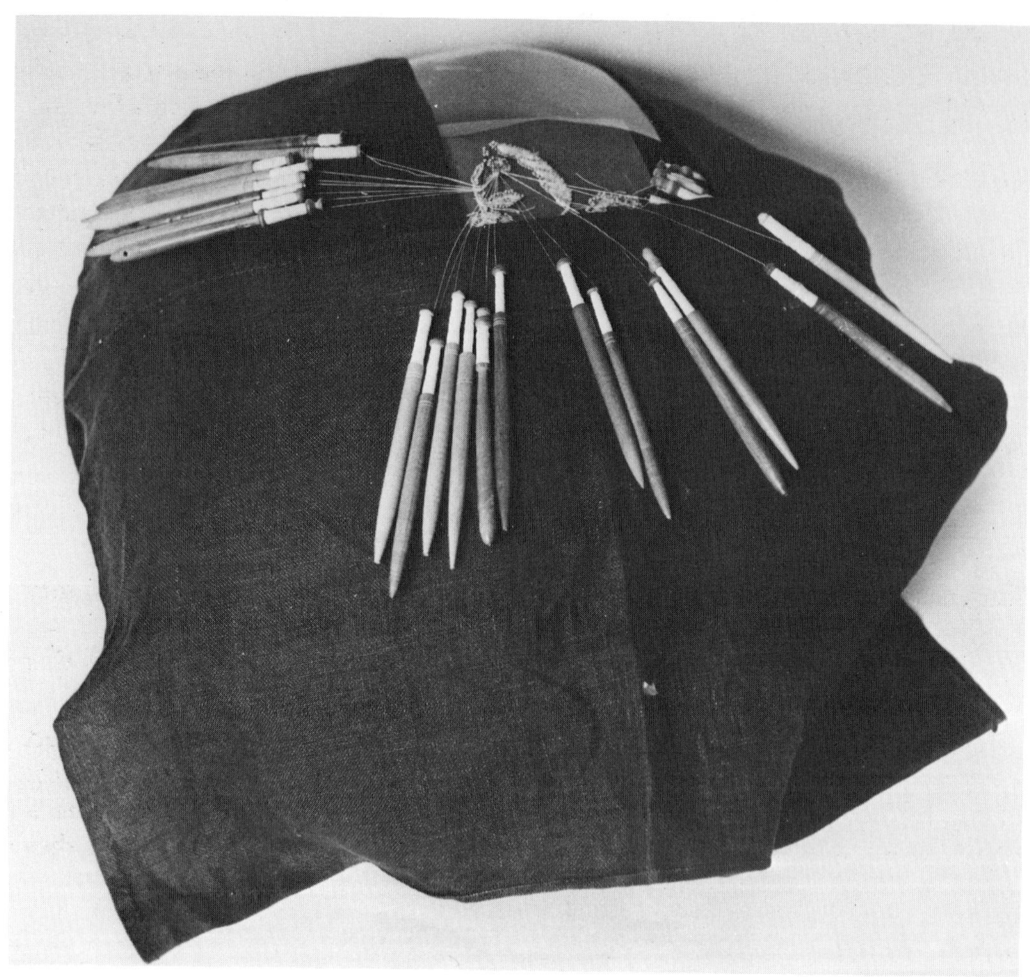

42. Honiton pillow

FLEMISH OR SWISS PILLOW

Other types are in existence notably that shown being used in the Flemish painting of *The Lace Maker* by Jan van der Meer. This is also a padded framed affair but instead of the bolster it has a wooden channel right down the middle holding 3 square padded wooden-based cushions that can be moved up as the work progresses and can also be lifted and turned for handkerchief and other corners. Instead of stuffing these 3 square cushions, which would give them a rounded effect, it is usual to fix on layers of thick felt to a depth of $\frac{3}{4}''$. See Photo 1 on title page. This pillow is best made on a board base but built up with fine-grained polystyrene of the kind used for packing electrical goods.

Another type is that seen (in many photos of workers) often called a mushroom. It is made from a square of material, the points brought to the middle, seamed and stuffed. It is heavy and therefore rather clumsy to use.

VARIOUS NOTES

When inspecting 'antique' pillows take a good look at the *used* middle. This may need attention involving re-stuffing.

The advantage of dark material for the under cloth and working cloth is that the holes of the pricking and the threads can be seen more easily.

Close grained polystyrene makes quite the best pillow in any shape, but it must be tightly covered with a very firm close woven cloth. Any worn part can be cut out and replaced, but I have not worn one out yet. Very few straw-filled can compare in pin holding qualities. Do *not* use ceiling tiles or similar alternatives as they are too soft.

Appendix B: The Pricking

A knowledge of the way the net is pricked is extremely valuable to the lacemaker. She will soon be able to prick her own patterns to suit her own purposes and it also enables her to find her way around traditional patterns and enlarge these to suit available threads.

Using ordinary graph paper first mark in the foot holes. These do *not* follow the diagonal lines of the net holes so it is best to get them in at the beginning. There are 2 lines of dots – 1 in the bottom corner of the outer square and the other in the top corner of the 2nd square at 1 in the diagram below. Now commence the net by dotting downwards on the next intersection at 2. Then a line of dots downwards $1\frac{1}{2}$ squares to the left at 3, thus forming parallelograms with the previous dots. Now place dots in the centre of this parallelogram at 4 coming just to the *right* of the graph line. While doing this always watch that this dot follows a diagonal line formed by the top right and bottom left dots. Then dot down at 5 on the intersection, placing the middle dots at 6 just to the *left* of the graph line. These diagonal rows of dots are at an angle of approximately 52°.

It is a good plan to dot out a good block of this net to keep permanently for use and re-use during pattern making using 10 to the inch graph paper.

When actually pricking your pattern, work with a fine needle (No. 9) in a handle of dowelling direct on the graph paper through to your pricking card, as this leads to greater accuracy than the use of pens, pencils and tracing paper. This fine work only has to be done once for each pattern and only for two or three repeats when you will have a *template* from which to prick the rest of the pricking. See Chapter 2 for the correct use of this small piece.

If you are using thread such as 120 cotton, a finer graph can of course be used. Twelve to the inch is a good size but the really fine old prickings use the equivalent of a square of 2 mm so that the oblong shape is 3 mm × 2 mm.

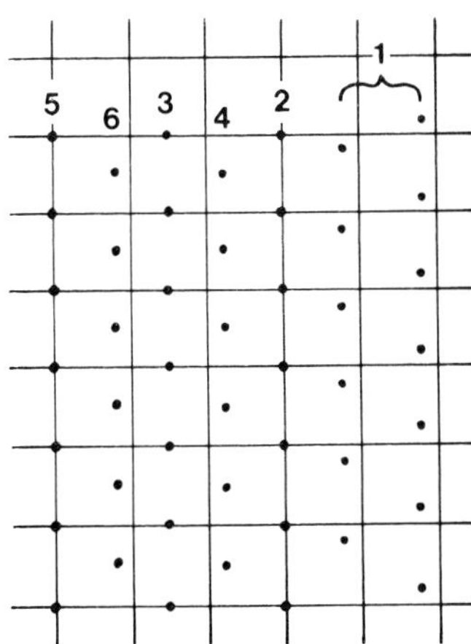

Diagram 54.
Point pricking

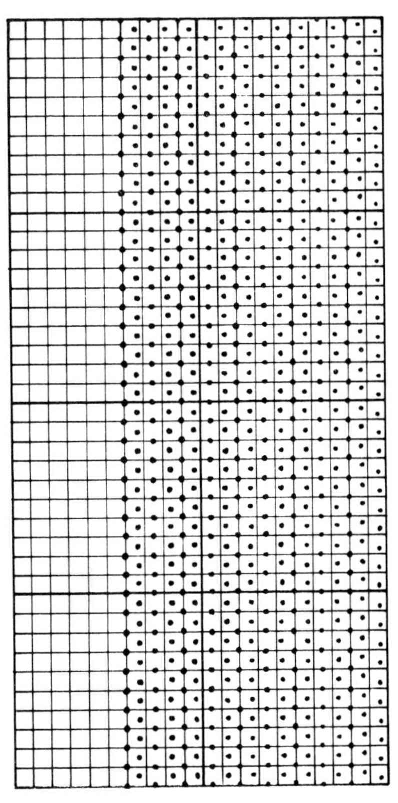

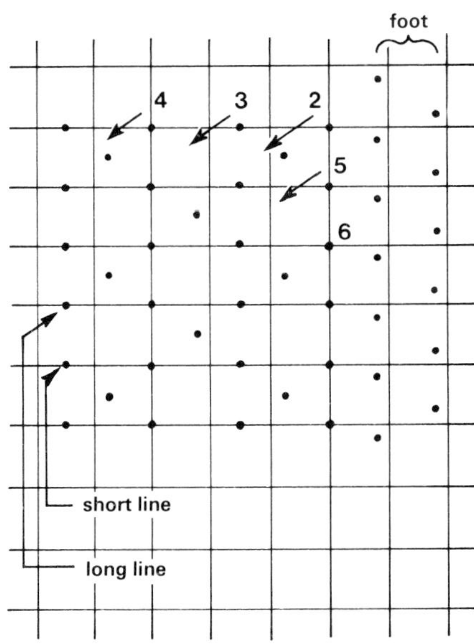

Diagram 55. Honeycomb

When pricking net I find it easier on the eyes to prick downwards 4 dots and then put in the centre ones containing 2 lines. Then return to the top of the pricking and do the next 2 lines similarly.

Honeycomb net is formed on the same base as the point ground but alternate lines have alternate dots left out, the alternate spaces thus formed arranged on the diagonal. It is easier to prick this on the diagonal lines, having first learnt the geography of the net. So that having done the foot, beginning at the top right-hand corner of the space to be filled prick a 'long line', i.e. a continual line of dots in every net place. Then do the *half-way* dot parallel with the first spot, working diagonally, miss centre spot, make the intersection dot, miss centre, dot the half-way one. At 4 do a 'long line' – all dots. Move to 5, begin with the intersection, miss centre dot, dot half-way one, miss centre, dot intersection, etc.

Note 1. The pricking now has a *perpendicular* line of intersection dots, a 'short' line missing alternately the centre dots to the right of the graph line, a line of half-way dots and a line of centre dots to the left of the graph line missing alternate dots to those on the previous line of centre dots.

Note 2. The diagonal short and long lines can be read and worked descending to the left as well as to the right which is a useful thing to remember when working out the making of the lace and direction of threads.

Note 3. When doing a corner it often *looks* as if this Hc pricking need not be turned to work across the corner. This is an error that has led to many muddled prickings and frustrated workers. The 52° angle must be remembered and the resulting diamond shape for the Hc must lie straight across the line of the pattern as in Diagram 56.

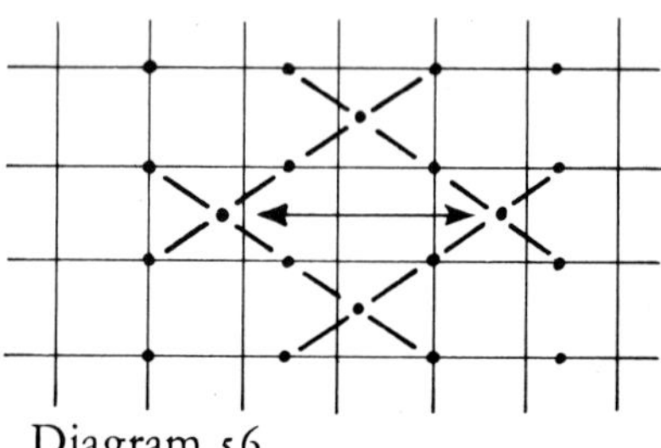

Diagram 56.

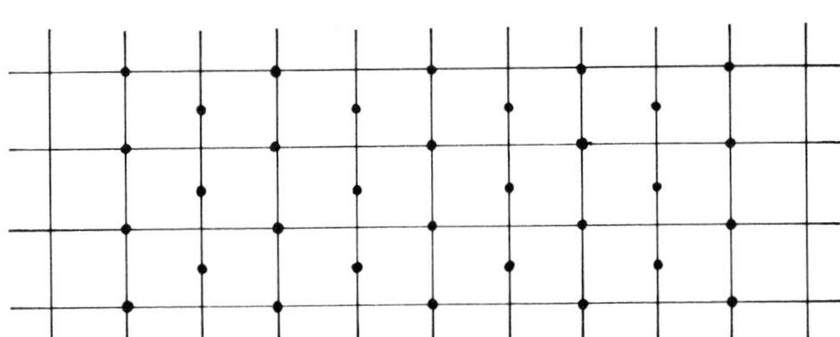

Diagram 57. Kat Stitch

FRENCH GROUND, KAT STITCH OR WIRE GROUND

This net can be used for the ground work or as a filling within other shapes. The diamond of the dots is longer horizontally, therefore the parallelogram used is formed by holes *on* every other intersection with the middle holes half way up the squares on the free line. The foot is pricked the same as the net and not moved slightly as in 'point'. For the working of Kat Stitch see Chapter 7.

BUDS AND HEADS, ETC.

As seen in cloth work in 'Little Fan', the Honeycomb of 'Sheep's Head', 'Duke's Garter' and similar regular patterns the pricking inside the shapes follows the pricking holes of the net leaving out the centre holes of the woven areas. See the diagrams in the chapters dealing with these laces. If the net lines are strictly adhered to, it is easy to see where the prs come in to and go out from these shapes.

In Floral and other indefinite shapes the inside pin holes of cloth work have sometimes to be adapted *slightly* where the lace may look thin without some extra prs. But do not do much of this wangle and always bear in mind that prs must come in and go out at the proper angles to keep the outside net regular and avoid holes developing at the edge of the shapes. When thickening is required, rather than depart from the proper holes in the right place it is better to hang extra prs on the workers at the side pin holes, remembering that these extra prs will have to be 'carried' with the gimp or in some similar way, or 'taken out' at the end of the shape which means cut ends left here and there.

HEAD PINS OR PURLS

The holes for these are pricked freehand about a square's width apart watching where they are to go in keeping the correct net angle (52°) as much as possible. The space between the purl pin hole and the inside lace hole must be wider than the net distances to allow for the gimp, the neck of the purl and several passive prs that may be coming out from the head or waiting to go in. Look at the 'Duke's Garter' where slightly more space is needed at the inner corner than at the outer edge.

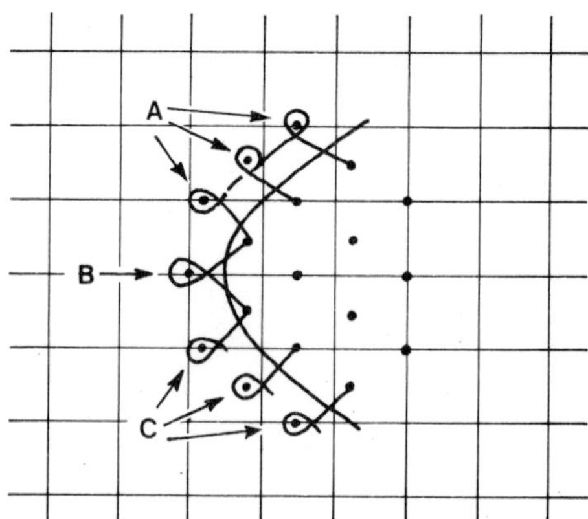

Diagram 58.
Head pins or Purls

When dotting in the *Head Pins* bear the above in mind. On a curve there will be places where the prs from the head will go in and work the lace at A, places where the purling pr will go in and come out once or several times as at B and, at the bottom of the curve at C, they will go out and stay out. So in the areas A and B passive prs are carried along outside the gimp and need space for the purlers to weave through. Note also when allocating space between head pins and gimp the problem noted in the diagram for 'Duke's Garter', page 40. Where there is a deep indent between heads the pairs outside the gimp tend to mount the corner pin in working so need anchoring flat by means of a twist or two before and after a wh st made with the pr coming out to the corner pin and the innermost passive, which is then used to go in to the next head. In pricking deep heads it is often necessary to have a Hc stitch in the depth of the V as also is the case in groups of Hc rings where it is sometimes more convenient to prick a Hc than to take the worker out to the head.

BOOKS

The following is a small selection of the best books on lace-making. There are many good books available and some that are currently out of print are worth looking for in libraries and second-hand bookshops.

History of Lace, Palliser (Sampson & Low)
Manual of Handmade Bobbin Lace, Maidment (Branford, USA)
Lace in the Making, Brook (Routledge)
Lace Making by Diagram, Nyrop Larson (Gjellerup Forlag, Copenhagen)
Pillow Lace, Mincoff and Marriage (Murray)
Point and Pillow Lace, A.M.S. (Murray)
Knyppleskan, Books I, II and III, Olsson (Holmqvist, Sweden)
Pillow Lace in the East Midlands, Freeman (Corporation of Luton)
Lace Making, Point Ground, Channer (Dryad of Leicester)
The Book of Bobbin Lace Stitches, Cook and Stott (Batsford)
The Technique of Honiton Lace, Luxton (Batsford)
The Technique of Bobbin Lace, Nottingham (Batsford)
The Technique of Bucks Point, Nottingham (Batsford)
Dentelles de Notre Temps, Elena Holeczyova (Dessain et Tolra, France)
Nyplättyä Pitsiä, Eeva-Liisa Kortelahti
Creative Design in Bobbin Lace, Collier (Batsford)

SUPPLIERS

There are now so many of these that only a few of the outstanding firms who supply the greatest variety of goods are listed here. Membership of the Lace Guild is useful as their quarterly magazine carries a large number of specialist advertisers.

D. J. Hornsby, 149 High Street, Burton Latimer, Kettering, Northants NN15 5RL (bobbins, threads, pins, pillows and a comprehensive book list)
Audrey Sells, Lane Cove, 49 Pedley Lane, Flifton, Shefford, Beds.
Bucks Bobbins, Woodside, Greenlands Lane, Prestwood, Great Missenden, Bucks.
Fireside Books, Ken & Pat Schulz, Coppins, Ixworth Road, Honington, Bury St Edmunds, Suffolk IP31 1QY (books and pillows)
David and Christen Springett, 251 Hillmorton Road, Rugby, Warwickshire
The English Lace School, 42 St Peter Street, Tiverton, Devon (antique lace, bobbins etc.)
Frederick J. Fawcett Inc., 129 South Street, Boston, Mass 02111, USA
Katie Kliott, Some Place, 2150 Stuart Street, Berkeley, CA 94705, USA
Manufacture Belge de Dentelles S.A., 6–8 Galerie de la Reine, Galerie Royale St Hubert, 1000 Bruxelles, Belgium